DAILY✠EXPRESS

buying & selling
PROPERTY

how to get the best deal on your home

sarah o'grady

KOGAN
PAGE

643.12

First published in Great Britain in 2003 by Kogan Page Limited

120 Pentonville Road
London N1 9JN
www.kogan-page.co.uk

© Express Newspapers 2003

British Library Cataloguing in Publication Data

A CIP record for this book is available from the British Library

ISBN 0 7494 3907 6

Typeset by Saxon Graphics Ltd, Derby
Printed and bound in Great Britain by Thanet Press Ltd, Margate

'*Chic, stylish and eclectic*' describe Onedeko, a contemporary home interiors shop located at Old Spitalfields market in London's trendy E1 area.

Described in a recent BBC '*Guide to Shopping in London*' as a '*must see*' where everything on display is '*ultimately desirable*', this recently expanded shop has much to offer. There is a wide variety of furniture (lounge and dining) and all sorts of household accessories from around the globe. Intermixed with this are innovative products from local designers. A growing art selection has recently clad the walls and in addition to the luxurious rugs on the floors, there is now a much more extensive range of lighting solutions – including free standing and wall mounted.

Watch out for equally original coffee tables, ranging from Backgammon to Neon Lit, and the cool remake of the classic Space Invaders table inclusive of full working PC and a jukebox. The most coveted product however is the Mascotte coffee/dining table. This is a stylish coffee table with a solid wood frame and veneered wood top. At the touch of a button it becomes a dining table for six, offering the perfect working and dining solution for even the smallest of London studios.

One of the benefits of Onedeko's recent showroom expansion is their new dining range that encompasses up to 30 dining tables, all of which extend or shorten in length. They come in a range of finishes from solid wood with veneered tops, to glass, chrome and metal. A range of dining chairs add an additional touch of Italian magic to the scene.

The shop has enjoyed a well earned run of publicity recently from various sources. Much of this has to do with a growing reputation for customer care and a furniture delivery time that is hard to beat. Their superb range of leather and fabric sofas, sofa beds and chairs are made to order and delivered straight to your door within four weeks. A bespoke service is available on all models so that standard sizes and dimensions can be tailored to suit the needs of each customer.

E1 has fast become a vibrant colourful alternative to the main shopping areas of London and Old Spitalfields Market is a great venue for a day out, Onedeko is located at 111A Commercial Street on the north eastern corner of the market. Call **0207 375 3289** for a free brochure or check out their website **www.onedeko.co.uk**

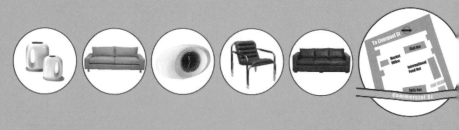

Contents

Introduction

Moving home is up there with death and divorce as one of the top causes of stress in our lives. Surveys and solicitor's fees aren't cheap and one mistake can cost you – literally – thousands of pounds.

The sheer physical effort of house-hunting, packing and unpacking, as you stumble through the UK's convoluted and old-fashioned system of purchasing property is likely to add grey hairs.

As buying or selling a home is likely to be the biggest financial transaction most of us are involved in, the stakes are high. Without careful planning or clear thought, buying a property can turn into a nightmare of gargantuan proportions.

This book, written in plain and simple language, aims to help you through the complicated maze that is the British property market. Whether you are a first-time buyer, a serial mover or an amateur landlord, you will, I hope, find the answers to most of your questions within these pages.

Sarah O'Grady
Property Editor, Express Newspapers

Buying and Selling Property

By taking a modern approach to storage, residents are effectively increasing the amount of living space in their existing homes, 'un-cluttering' their lives and making the absolute most of their modern urban lifestyles. In some cases, they have even avoided the need to make the costly, disruptive move to a larger property.

Whether it's for people storing furniture during a home renovation, moving from a large house in the country to 'city living' or just de-cluttering to make more space in the home, more and more people are demanding high quality, clean, dry and secure storage facilities that they can operate and control themselves.

The UK's leading personal storage company, Spaces Personal Storage, which has 44 facilities around the country, is finding a sustained growth in demand for its services, as Operations Director Andrew Burleigh, explains:

"The personal storage concept has come over to Europe from the United States. It is basically about hiring space to store virtually anything and customers in the UK are fast becoming aware of the benefits and advantages to be gained in this way.

"The trend towards minimalist living is also benefiting our business. Self-storage is no longer simply just about storing furniture during a home move, but also storing valuable but 'not wanted now' furniture for the future."

"It's also about modern urban living and lifestyles," he says. "More and more people are recognising that they can enjoy their living space to the full by removing clutter from their homes which avoids having to sell or throw away valued possessions."

"Although homeowners, who are in the process of buying and selling, are not the only customers to take advantage of the self-storage concept they are a core area of our business. Their needs can vary from vendors moving into temporary accommodation and avoiding the collapse of property chains to homeowners using new marketing techniques such as de-personalising and de-cluttering the home to encourage sales."

According to Channel 5's 'House Doctor' Ann Maurice, the use of personal storage in order to get all of the clutter out of the home, not only makes the house look considerably bigger, but also enables the potential purchaser to visualise their furniture and possessions in the house.

"The obvious things like tidying up and making the house look clean and neat are not necessarily the best possible approach any more," says Ann Maurice. "Certainly the house should be clean and tidy, but by editing one's possessions such as clothes, toys, books, ornaments, even furniture and putting all excess into storage during the selling period, a seller is likely to achieve much better results in terms of first impressions and saleability."

The centres are all secure with CCTV systems, alarms, controlled access and security lighting and many of them now offering 24hr direct access units. Spaces also offer a range of unit sizes from the traditional locker size for small items, right up to thousands of square feet units.

The cost for storing the contents of an average three bedroom house at the Spaces centre in central Birmingham, for example, is £131.20 a month.

For more information about Spaces Personal Storage call free phone **0800 62 22 44** or visit **www.spaces.uk.com**

If you haven't got space, you've always got Spaces.

- In a chain or stuck for somewhere to store until you move house? • Just need somewhere to store clutter, hobby gear, business assets or need to create more living room? • Then talk to one of our nationwide Spaces Personal Storage centres • Spaces self-storage units range from 8 sq ft to over 3,000 sq ft. • CCTV protected, electronic security with you the only keyholder • Free use of pallet trucks and trolleys • No hidden charges for access • Insurance packages available • Very competitive prices • For a full list of all 44 centres, locations and packaging products, a virtual tour and all current discount offers, check out **www.spaces.uk.com** now or **FREEPHONE 0800 62 22 44** (answered 24 hours a day).

spaces ◆ personal storage

Self-storage rooms to rent for the home and business.

1

Can you afford to buy and what are the first steps?

For many people, the question, 'Can I afford to buy my own home?' really should be: 'Can I afford *not* to buy?'

Renting is fine if interest rates are high or threaten to rise steeply, or if you have other doubts about your future career path. Compared to renting, however, buying a property makes more economic sense in the long-term.

Issues to consider

The following are some key points to consider:

- How much is the mortgage compared to the cost of renting?
- At what level would interest rates have to rise for renting to make more sense?
- How much more would I have to pay in terms of household and other insurance, annual maintenance costs, service charges (where applicable) and any other costs?
- What are the up-front costs of buying (legal and mortgage application fees, surveys, stamp duty)?
- If I am taking out an interest-only loan, could I afford to pay into a separate investment plan to pay off the loan itself?
- Am I going to lose any flexibility to move – perhaps to further a career or travel?

Of course, people buy and sell for all kinds of reasons, not just because it's economically a better deal. Sometimes, as the bills and fees mount up, it is obviously not.

While I am strongly in favour of owning my own home – along with more than 70 per cent of the UK population that does so – I am not in favour of personal bankruptcy. If you can save a larger deposit while paying rent for a few months longer, then do so. That will save you more money in the long run – as the bigger the deposit, the less interest you pay – and will give you a greater choice of property when you start looking around.

How difficult can it be?

Listening to the conversation at any dinner party, a novice buyer can be forgiven for thinking that buying a property is easy. Simply find the right house, spend the most money you've ever spent on what will probably be your biggest purchase ever and wait for move-in day. Right? Wrong.

As those of us who have had our fingers burnt – sometimes more than once – know, buying your own home can be a supremely satisfying achievement. Or, it can be a most frustrating, disappointing, stressful, emotional and expensive episode. The secret between one and the other lies in proper prior planning.

Proper prior planning

Don't walk into any old estate agent's office on the High Street, arrange to view and then make an offer on the first place you see. Ask around for local recommendations of agents in the area you want to move to.

Visit the ones that have been recommended. How do they strike you? Are they members of the National Association of Estate Agents (NAEA). Membership of the NAEA means they have signed up to a Code of Practice and professional Rules of Conduct. This does not guarantee good service or honest dealing, but does give you some leverage if things go wrong. Many reputable agents also belong to the Ombudsman for Estate Agents (OEA) scheme.

Remember that an estate agent works for the seller – not you. They earn their commission by helping owners to sell. A reputable and professional agent should always answer your questions truthfully, but they are not obliged to tell you anything negative about the property. That's why you need a good solicitor.

Also, look at the adverts in the local papers – an agent with the wit to run a polished advertising campaign is a better bet than one who places a few grainy photos. While you're in these branches, take away as many details about as many properties in your price range as possible. Study them so you get a good idea of what's on offer and at what kind of price.

Find out how much you can borrow

Arrange at least a couple of appointments with mortgage lenders. Start with the bank or building society you bank with. There's a relationship there already and they have all your financial details to hand.

You need to know exactly how much they will lend you and what kind of deal they will give you. Don't be afraid of asking questions or trying to negotiate a better deal. Competition between lenders is intense. Exploit it. Don't stick with one lender if another is likely to offer you more favourable terms.

There's no charge, so see as many as you like. Don't let them sell you anything – insurance etc – as there's plenty of time before you're likely to make an offer. Take copious notes.

Also, read the money and personal finance pages of the newspapers. They have up-to-the-minute details of all the latest mortgage offers.

Viewing

Now you're ready to view, there are three golden rules:

- Don't waste the estate agent's time.
- Don't waste the seller's time.
- Don't waste your own time.

If you want a garden flat and the agent offers you a top-floor apartment, don't bother going to see it. If you start by seeing absolutely everything, you'll find yourself harassed and disappointed. Stick within the remit you've set the agent.

Do try and have some idea about the kind of property you're looking for. The agent needs to have some boundaries to work within. If he takes you to see ten or so and you're never interested, he's going to write you off as a waste of time and concentrate on other clients where he's more likely to get a sale.

Questions to ask yourself

The following questions might be useful in narrowing your choice:

- Do you want a house or a flat?
- Do you want an old property or a new one?
- Do you care if the home is leasehold or freehold? Freehold means you own the land on which the house stands and most houses are freehold. Leasehold means you have a lease on a property for a number of years (you can buy properties with leases of just 15 years, but most are hundreds of years long), which is sold to you by the freeholder of the land. That means you own the property but not the land. Most flats, for example, are leasehold.
- Where do you want to live?
- Do you want a garden?
- Do you need parking?
- Do you need to be close to public transport?
- How many bedrooms do you want?
- Do you want to renovate the building or do you want to be able to move straight in?
- How long are you planning to live in it? Is it suitable if your circumstances change, ie if you have children or an elderly parent moves in?

It's both a strength and a weakness of the way we buy and sell property in England and Wales that a buyer can withdraw right up to the last minute. That's not the case in Scotland where contracts are signed much earlier in the proceedings. But to deliberately string a seller along if you have no real intention of buying is not honourable. Treat others as you would wish to be treated. If you're buying now the chances are that you will be a seller in the future.

Questions to ask the seller

You should ask the seller as many questions as possible when viewing:

- Why are you moving?
- How long has the property been on the market?
- Is it chain-free?
- What are you leaving behind? Are you expecting payment for some of the fixtures, ie carpets?
- How much are the average utility bills?
- How much is the council tax?
- How much is the service charge or ground rent?
- What are the neighbours like?
- Have you ever been burgled?
- Have you made any improvements to the property? Have you got the guarantees and warranties?
- How easy is it to park? Do I need a permit? How much do they cost?
- What are the local schools like?
- Is it a Neighbourhood Watch area?
- What are the local transport links?
- What local amenities – libraries, shops, surgeries – are there?

Finding a solicitor or licensed conveyancer

So you've found a couple of estate agents you trust, you know how much you can borrow and you're viewing properties. Now find a solicitor or licensed conveyancer to handle any purchase for you.

The best way is by word-of-mouth. Unless you already have a family solicitor, a personal recommendation is worthwhile having. Someone local to the area in which you want to buy is also a good idea, as they will have a better idea of council planning polices or restrictions.

The Law Society, the National Solicitors' Network or the Council for Licensed Conveyancers will also supply you with a list of people practising in your area. Your mortgage lender may also give you a couple of names. Again, you don't have to sign up to anything immediately. You simply want to find someone you trust to do a good job and know how much they're likely to charge in advance of any offer you might make.

Buying a home in England and Wales takes twice as long as in the rest of Europe. Pitfalls such as gazumping – the seller accepting a higher offer after they have already accepted yours – or gazundering – a buyer threatening to withdraw at the last minute unless the seller reduces the price – litter the way.

Proper prior planning means you know what you're talking about and gives you an edge in terms of time. If you have your finances and solicitor sorted out in advance, you can move quicker than your competitors, thereby reducing the risk of losing your dream house.

2

Finding the right area

Finding the right area to live is now far easier than it used to be. With new online services you can compare everything from house prices to a local school's results in seconds.

Issues to consider

When you start looking for a new home there are various factors that could affect your choice of where to live. The list below covers the main considerations.

Schools

If you have a young family, getting your children into the right school can determine the area you choose. Beware, though: school catchment areas are not clearly defined. Check with your estate agent exactly what 'in the vicinity of' (a typical agent's blurb) actually means – and confirm that with the school itself.

Council tax

Living in some areas can seem attractive until the council tax bill comes in and you discover that, in addition to the mortgage, you have to find a further £500–£600 a year. Sometimes it would make more sense to look at a property just a few streets away from your preferred location.

If you think your tax is too high, write to the council immediately. Challenging a council tax valuation on your property is generally possible only shortly after purchase, although there may be exceptions.

As from this year, 2003, the 50 per cent rebate on council tax for second homeowners will be scrapped and owners will be liable for up to 90 per cent of the local rate.

Services

Not only can council taxes be high, services such as rubbish collection, road mending, sports facilities and parks may be inadequate. Check them out, together with other amenities, such as cinemas, shops and restaurants. Decide whether they meet your current and likely future needs.

Transport

Transport links are an important consideration. Prices are usually lower in areas with poor links, but that is not an inviolable rule. If you are buying in London, check the boundaries of the new Congestion Charge.

Crime

A home can turn into a prison if you live in a heavily crime-ridden area. Find out from your local police station what the crime statistics are or look at the local authority website. Talk to local shopkeepers to learn more. Consider personal safety issues, such as whether this is an area you would feel comfortable walking around at night or when coming home from work.

House prices

In the past couple of years, parts of the UK have seen spectacular rises in property values. Other areas of the country have languished. Many big cities have seen double-digit price increases, while others have stood still.

Your first need is for a roof over your head. But after that, there's nothing wrong with trying to find the latest hotspot.

To find a future hotspot, where prices are set to rise faster than average, check for emerging developments in the area. For example, is it close to another area that is over-heating where you might benefit from over-spill purchases? Are new transport links planned?

How to buy a home in a sought-after area

If your heart is set on moving into a particular neighbourhood, you may find that you are not the only one who absolutely must have a home there.

For whatever reason, be it the best schools, the nicest streets, the choice of restaurants on the doorstep or the exclusive postcode, sought-after areas present a real challenge to the house hunter and proper prior planning is the key.

Networking

Before a property ever makes it as far as the estate agent's shop window or newspaper advertisement, it's been seen by a huge number of people. Some properties in areas of high demand never even appear on the open market, as professional house hunters and corporate relocation agents make it their business to be on the agent's priority list, so they get the inside track on new properties coming up for sale. You, too, need to make those kind of contacts, so that if a desirable property comes on the market you get an early tip-off.

Visit the local estate agents to introduce yourself. Find the one or two who deal most in the kind of property you want to buy in the area you like. Make sure the agents know you are not a time-waster. Impress upon them that you are a serious buyer with the ability to move quickly if the right kind of property comes up. Telephone or drop in regularly so they have your face and requirements in mind as new homes come on the market.

Check what day the property pages are published in the local paper. It may be possible that the newsagent can forward them on to you. Check out the local property website.

Visit the area regularly. You may find For Sale boards being put up that day, or people moving out.

Mail shot the houses in the neighbourhood you want to move into. If you have a PC and printer, it is easy to knock up a leaflet. Posting, say, 80 of them on a Saturday morning might turn up a surprising result and even if the house owner isn't moving, they may know someone who is.

Preparation

As soon as you have made the decision to move and found the right area, do as much preparation as possible. Good preparation will enable you to make better decisions about properties and move quicker.

Make a wish list of what you want from a property, the features you must have and the things you can live without. This will help focus your mind on the types of property you want and help you filter out those properties that you could get carried away with.

Arrange a provisional mortgage offer first and start talking to a solicitor. The more paperwork you have sorted out, the quicker you can proceed when your offer has been accepted.

Viewings

You must be ready to move quickly in sought-after areas. If an agent calls and says 'I've just had this wonderful flat come on the market', you need to be able to say, 'Great, I'm on the way.' Failing that, make arrangements for someone whose opinion you trust to do the viewing, perhaps with a camcorder if you have access to one, so you can view the pictures later. Take a notebook with you to make notes. Try and imagine the room without the seller's furniture in it. Look at the physical aspects of the property – not the seller's taste. Are the rooms large enough? Do they get enough light? Is there room to extend the kitchen, etc?

What kind of property do you want?

Buying old

Many of us harbour a love of older houses with their in-built character. Whether they are Edwardian villas in the city or listed Georgian rectories in the country, these kinds of properties are sought-after, as generations of new owners imagine the lives of the people who lived in the house before them.

The best of the UK's older properties – 550,000 of them ranging from cottages to castles – are classified as part of the country's heritage and are listed Grade I, Grade II* and Grade II.

All buildings built before 1700 that survive in anything like their original condition are automatically listed, as are many built in the 18th, 19th and even the 20th century.

Properties are listed because:

- they are of special architectural interest;
- they are of special historical interest;
- they have close historical associations with nationally important events or people;
- they have special historical or architectural importance as a group of buildings;
- they are considered to be of outstanding design or quality; or
- they mark a pinnacle of building fashion or standards.

The most important structures are listed Grade I, including Windsor Castle and the Houses of Parliament, and there are nearly 9,000 of them. But if you are lucky enough to be thinking of buying a Grade I listed building, do bear in mind that ownership comes with responsibilities and restrictions. Nothing can be done to alter the building and all repairs have to be carried out in keeping with the original. Because of this, repairs and maintenance can be cripplingly expensive. In some cases, however, grants are available from English Heritage to help with the cost.

Grade II is the commonest classification and there are 350,000 Grade II listed buildings in the country. Here, too, owners face restrictions and have to get special consent for alterations to the property.

Local authorities sometimes give grants towards repair work on listed buildings and you save on VAT, which is zero-rated for improvements on approved alterations.

If you fancy owning a piece of history, contact Save Britain's Heritage or the Society for the Protection of Ancient Buildings. In Scotland, contact the Scottish Civic Trust.

Buying new

New homes are increasing in popularity as developers shrug off their old reputations for boring, box-like homes built without character or style, and build exciting, innovative homes for families in the 21st century.

A new home has all kinds of advantages: high-tech heating and lighting systems, high security, luxurious fixtures and fittings, modern plumbing and all 'mod cons' in the bathrooms and kitchens.

If you get in to a new development early enough – perhaps by buying 'off-plan' before the property is even built – many developers offer buyers the opportunity to choose their own fixtures, fittings and colour schemes.

You must make sure though, that you buy a property that has been built by one of the 20,000 companies that are members of the National House Building Council (NHBC), or those that are members of the Zurich Municipal Scheme, which means that the building of the property is insured against the developer going bankrupt. Major defects found in the first two years will also be put right.

There are very few lenders who will give you a mortgage on a property that is not built by an NHBC or Zurich builder or under the supervision of a properly insured architect or surveyor.

There are a few things worth bearing in mind if you are buying a new-build home.

We build everywhere – but not just anywhere.

As one of the UK's leading housebuilders, Persimmon provides quality homes the length and breadth of the country. But no matter the area, we always take as much care selecting the exact location as we do in the actual construction. Before a single brick is laid we'll ensure there's everything a potential buyer could wish for. From excellent transport links through to local amenities, from attractive surroundings through to sympathetic architecture – we strive to choose only those spots which offer the homebuyer more. To find out about the Persimmon development in the area you're interested in, please visit our website at **www.persimmonhomes.co.uk**

PERSIMMON
Together, we make a home

Whether you're a first time buyer or a seasoned mover, the first step towards finding your dream home is deciding whether to buy an old or new property.

As one of the UK's leading housebuilders, Persimmon is well qualified to point out the pros and cons.

Whilst for some, there's no substitute for wooden beams, unusual shaped rooms and uneven walls, many purchasers take on the history of an older property without fully appreciating the often hidden costs associated with turning it into their dream home. And even if an older property doesn't require significant modernisation, running costs are likely to be higher.

Buying a new home has a number of obvious advantages – no maintenance, no accumulation of 'someone else's' dreaded dirt, no decorating disasters to put right.

Energy efficient gas central heating, modern insulation and PVCu double glazing are also standard on most new homes ensuring that costs are kept to a minimum.

However, there are other, less obvious, benefits which may be worth considering.

Most developers offer purchasers the opportunity to buy their new home 'off plan" - that is, before it has been built. With detailed site layouts, artists illustrations and even 'virtual' walk throughs available to enable purchasers to visualise their brand new homes, buying off plan offers significant advantages.

For instance, additional features can be added to the home at this stage with the minimum of fuss and expense. You can also choose the colour and style of standard features such as kitchen units work surfaces and tiles and bathroom tiles.

And to enable purchasers to stamp their own individual style on their new home, Persimmon offers a wide range of 'Finishing Touches' – a unique range of sales extras which allows purchasers to add or upgrade selected items from a range including ceramic flooring, stainless steel appliances, interior designed curtains, landscaped gardens, alarm systems, fitted carpets, feature fireplaces, conservatory, choice of wall colour and additional BT/TV/powerpoints.

Location is a primary consideration when moving home and if you're moving to a new area, a new home is sometimes the best choice. Modern housing developments are designed to foster a sense of community and with everyone moving in at around the same time, getting to know your neighbours can often be easier than in an already established community.

Buying new has many other advantages, with developers providing every assistance to ensure that moving home is a enjoyable experience. For example, Persimmon has recently invested in the new Persimmon 'Masterfile' – an indispensable housebuying handbook, carefully compiled to guide purchasers through every step of the housebuying process from reservation through exchange of contracts to a relaxed and hassle-free moving in day.

The handbook is split into four sections, each containing concise and easy-to-use information about everything from instructing a solicitor to what to do in case of an emergency, plus information on the purchasers' specific development and checklists for every stage of the housebuying process. It even contains change of address cards and practical suggestions for what to pack in a moving in survival kit including toys for the children, remote controls for any electrical appliances, champagne (and glasses)!

The Masterfile offers help and advice for every step of the moving process and is the latest addition to the Persimmon package, which now includes a full range of services including financial advice, mortgages, help for first time buyers and a tailored interior design service.

In practical terms, Persimmon can also offer help to purchasers stuck in a chain, and on some homes, help out with legal costs and provide assistance with selling an existing property. A range of incentives is also available on selected properties to enable first time buyers to take their first step onto the property ladder.

All new Persimmon homes benefit from a 10 year NHBC guarantee, providing purchasers with the assurance that their new home meets stringent quality standards.

Founded in 1972 by Group Chairman Duncan Davidson, Persimmon is one of the UK's largest homebuilders, constructing in excess of 12,500 homes per year on approximately 350 developments nation-wide.

With its headquarters in York, the group comprises North and South divisions with a total of 24 regional offices building from Scotland through the North, East and Midlands, down to the South and South West of England and South Wales.

Specialist company Persimmon City Developments aims to bring life back into Britain's cities through the innovative redevelopment of carefully selected urban land with key developments in London, Newcastle, Glasgow, Edinburgh, Birmingham and Bristol.

Persimmon specialises in offering a wide choice of beautifully designed homes in prime locations throughout the UK. Whether a studio apartment or executive family home, Persimmon has a reputation for building properties of the highest quality.

For further information, please contact the Persimmon hotline on 08459 10 10 11 or visit the company online at www.persimmonhomes.com

- Check the builder's reputation and look at houses he has built before.
- Is he a member of the NHBC? If so, the property qualifies for the Corporation's 10-year Buildmark Cover after completion. Ring 0845 845 6422 to check.
- Visit the site. Is it tidy, clean, safe and well managed? This will give you a sign of the developer's commitment to quality.
- Is there a 'Pride in the Job' award-winning mark on site boards? This is another sign that the new homes are being built with quality workmanship.
- Before completion check with your solicitor that the property has received its certificate from the NHBC.
- Think about getting a home-buyer's or structural survey done.
- Check the history of the land use.
- If you do have problems within the first two years, put your complaint in writing.

The House Builders Federation promotes new homes and can provide a list of developers working in the area you want to move into. Their website is www.hbf.co.uk or try www.new-homes.co.uk.

Buying eco-friendly

House buyers may soon benefit from tax breaks and cheaper properties under a deal to promote 'green homes' being considered by the Government. Ministers are examining proposals that one million UK homes be classified as 'sustainable' by 2012.

The tax incentives are one route being looked at to persuade developers to create new or renovated eco-friendly homes. These would include innovations like:

- reduced running costs through greater energy and water efficiency, and reduced maintenance;
- healthy internal environments;
- access to local amenities and less dependence on car usage;

Do you know what your house is built on?

Don't Buy More than Your Bargained For

The house you want to buy may look perfect but how much do you really know about the surrounding area or the land the property is built on? Do you know if your new home is built on a former industrial site that may have left contamination in the ground? Is there a planning application to build a supermarket in the adjoining field? Could your home be at risk from flooding? These are just some of the important questions you should consider when buying a new home.

The consequences of buying a property affected by environmental risks can be serious and expensive. Your property value can be substantially reduced if the land it's built on is contaminated, liable to flooding or affected by other environmental risks. Whilst serious problems are rare, it now costs so little to check on a whole series of potential problems that many homebuyers are asking their solicitor for an environmental search as a matter of course.

Your solicitor will usually undertake a local search as part of the conveyancing process but this will not tell you anything about environmental problems or future developments in the locality that could affect the property. In order to protect your investment and to avoid any nasty surprises it's worth asking your solicitor or licensed conveyancer to commission an Envirosearch and Plansearch report.

Envirosearch, approved by the NHBC, provides essential information on environmental risks including landfill and waste sites, contamination, polluting processes, hazardous substances, radioactive substances, mining activity, subsidence, flooding, radon and transmitters. Envirosearch also includes a surveyor's opinion that comments on whether the property value is likely to be affected by land contamination. Additionally Envirosearch provides a contaminated land insurance option to protect against unknown risks from contamination.

Plansearch provides homebuyers with details of current and historical planning applications for the property and the surrounding area. The report also provides details on future planning proposals in your neighbourhood as well as flood risk information. This report goes much further than the standard local authority search, which provides planning information just on an individual property.

Envirosearch and Plansearch will help any homebuyer to make an informed decision about purchasing a property and whether it will provide a suitable environment and investment for their family. Envirosearch is priced £39 and Plansearch costs £30 however you can save yourself £10 if you order both reports together. A small price to pay for peace of mind.

- what materials and resources are used in construction and routine household activities;
- the impact on local wildlife.

Whilst it would be unrealistic to call for a million new sustainable homes in 10 years, thanks to ever-improving technology such as solar panels, more efficient boilers, and energy-efficient timber windows, existing homes can be adapted to decent environmental standards at relatively modest cost. The government's Building Research Establishment has been working with conservationists and developers, and has developed an inspection and rating system for new and renovated homes.

'Eco-friendly' on estate agents' details usually means large and expensive, but more modestly-priced properties are now embracing green features. High-level insulation, triple-glazed windows with low-emission glass, and ventilation using recycled 'hot air' are being fitted as standard to many new homes.

You can even give listed buildings a green make-over. A Grade II-listed, four-storey Georgian terraced house in Bath was recently turned into five environmentally-friendly flats. Sash windows were fitted with concealed draught proofing, the roof insulated with lambswool, leaded windows were adapted to provide ventilation to areas with condensation, and piping buried beneath stone flags was lagged with polystyrene. It shows what can be done even with listed buildings. Projects like this transform the image of eco-friendly properties. Perhaps building new homes will not cost the Earth after all.

Staying put

Perhaps you are already living in the perfect location. And the house was once perfect too – though now it's little small, as your family grows or grandma moves in. In this case, moving isn't always the best option. When you add up the costs of buying and selling – stamp duty usually being the biggest bill – it often makes sense to stay put and build up, out, or even down.

While having the builders in for weeks or even months can be stressful, as can living on a building site, after the money has been spent and the work finished, most homeowners have the satisfaction of the extra space they wanted and an increase in the value of their property.

The best extensions, in terms of adding value, are bigger dining kitchens and family rooms, according to research by one high street estate agent. Extra bedrooms or an en suite bathroom also make the money back.

Another good value extension is the addition of a granny annexe. No matter how small, buyers later on feel they are getting two properties for the price of one and an annexe has the added advantage of being something that could be let out for extra income.

Extending your current property

Here are some guidelines should you decide to extend:

- Consult the local planning authority, who will tell you if you need planning permission. If your home is listed or in a conservation area it will be subject to more restrictive planning laws. You may be able to extend your house without need for planning permission under permitted development rights, but you must check. The Department of the Environment publishes a free booklet, *Planning Permission – A Guide for Householders,* available at council offices.
- Look at extensions and conversions at neighbours' homes and ask for recommendations and the numbers of the people who carried out the work. Get several quotes from different architects, surveyors or builders.
- Once you have the plans, approach several reputable building firms (if your surveyor/architect is not doing this for you), get estimates and choose one. All building work must meet building regulations and standards and is monitored by the local planning department. The quality of the building work will be examined as will health and safety, services and fire precautions. The Building Controls Officer

can demand extra foundations, more drainage, heavier beams, etc, and his requirements will have to be complied with.

- How are you going to finance the project? Do you need a loan or a further advance on your mortgage? When calculating costs include the construction expense, new fittings and furnishings and any temporary accommodation. Always overestimate. Check if you are eligible for any home improvement grants.

- Plan how long the work will take. Tie the architect/surveyor/builder down to a contract that includes full details of price and a guarantee as to when the work will start and finish. See if you can include a clause that means they lose money if the work is not finished by a certain date.

- Can you live on site? Do you have to? Most builders will move along faster without you on site, but regular visits to monitor progress are a must.

- Make sure you have all the correct letters of authority and guarantees for any work you have carried out. They may be necessary when you come to sell. And even if you don't plan on doing the work, it can sometimes add value to your property if you have already obtained planning permission for a conversion or alteration.

3

What can I afford?

Many buyers tend to think that what they can borrow and what they can afford are one and the same thing. They aren't.

Work out your budget

Your lender may be willing to lend you a vast amount of money, but the real question is: could you afford to pay it back every month, no matter what happens to interest rates? And have you taken into account the additional costs involved in owning a property?

The best way to work out what you can afford is to add up all the costs associated with home ownership. They break down into two basic components: one-off costs involved in buying the home itself and the ongoing costs of looking after it.

How the costs stack up

Solicitor's fees

If you are buying for the first time or remortgaging your current property, you will have to pay for a solicitor. Some mortgage deals offer to pay your legal costs, up to a certain limit. You will also have to pay the lender's costs involved in the mortgage process. Solicitors and Licensed Conveyancers can charge what they like. Their governing body, the Law Society, says fees should be 'fair and reasonable', based on factors like how much the property is worth, how much work, skill or time is necessary, the place and the circumstance of the conveyancing, whether the land is registered or unregistered, and how important the transaction is to the client.

Do get quotes from more than one conveyancer. The combined cost, including local authority searches, other payments, cash transfers and VAT can add up to more than £1,000 for an expensive home purchase, less outside London or for simpler transactions. Buying and selling at the same time may cost more.

Stamp duty

Stamp duty is a tax on already taxed income levied by the Inland Revenue on property purchases. It's also known as a tax on mobility and can cost you thousands of pounds just to change your address. It has to be paid when you complete your purchase.

For a property costing up to £60,000, there is no stamp duty. Once the price goes above £60,000, stamp duty is charged at one per cent up to £250,000, three per cent between £250,000 and £500,000 and four per cent thereafter. The charge is payable on the full purchase price. For example, a £700,000 house would involve stamp duty of £28,000.

Estate agent fees

If you have sold your home through an estate agent you will be expected to pay his fee on completion. This can vary from one to three per cent of the price (plus VAT). If you have sold, or are planning to sell, your property yourself, you will also have to factor in advertising rates.

Land Registry fees

These are payable – like stamp duty – on a scale related to the purchase price of the property.

Price of house	Land Registry fee
£0–£40,000	£40
£40,001–£70,000	£70
£70,001–£100,000	£100
£100,001–£200,000	£200
£200,001–£500,000	£300
£500,001–£1,000,000	£500
£1,000,001–£5,000,000	£800

Local authority searches

These are fees payable to local authorities and councils for information about any kind of construction in the area you want to buy a house. Your solicitor has to carry out these searches to find out, for example, if a new by-pass is planned at the bottom of the property's garden, or if planning permission has been granted for a housing estate nearby. The average cost is £65.

There are other searches and payments – company searches, land charges and bank transfer fees, to name but a few – which may have to be budgeted for too. Allow £75 for these to cover the average house purchase.

Sellers' packs

The packs, which could become compulsory in 2006, would contain title documents, replies to standard enquiries, copies of all planning, listed building and building regulation approvals and consents, a draft contract, local authority searches and a home condition report. They are expected to cost an average of £700.

Mortgage redemption charge

If you are moving and therefore repaying the original mortgage, there may be what the lender calls a Mortgage Redemption charge. This is usually calculated on a scale of how long you have had the mortgage. It could be up to three months interest. Check your contract. The lender may try to collect an 'administration' fee too.

Surveys

A surveyor's report on the general state of the property is a pre-requisite for lenders and most will not offer mortgages without one. Most banks and building societies offer a choice of three different types of survey – a valuation, a house-buyer's report or a full structural survey.

A structural survey will cost between £300 and £1,200 (plus VAT). There could also be additional costs for drainage checks or an inspection by a CORGI-registered heating engineer.

The house-buyer's report is less detailed and the fee, usually connected to the price of the property, would be between £250 and £350 for a £100,000 home.

The valuation is even less detailed and basically lets the lender know whether or not the property is worth the money you have offered. The cost depends on the value of the property and for under £100,000 would be around £200 but is occasionally carried out free by the lender as part of the mortgage package.

Application fees

Many lenders charge application fees of between £200 and £400 per mortgage application. Some charge even more. Watch out – sometimes this money is payable even when the application fails or is withdrawn.

Service charges

Before you buy a flat, or even a new house on a prestigious development, check the annual service charge. This is usually the annual cost of maintenance, repair, redecoration and insurance shared between owners. But service charges vary widely. Two apartment blocks may be part of the same residential complex, built at the same time, and look identical – except that the annual service charge for one is thousands of pounds greater than for the other. Always find out first what you are letting yourself in for.

Moving expenses

There is no greater misery than moving home yourself. It doesn't matter how much preparation and planning you have done, it's incredibly hard and time-consuming work. Sometimes there's no choice but to hire a van and get on with it, perhaps with the help of some willing friends and family. But if you can budget for the cost of using a professional removal firm, it is money well spent.

Always get several different quotations and ask for a breakdown of their services. Will they wrap and pack, or do they just collect and drop? And check they are insured.

If you have to do it yourself, you have to factor in the cost of the van (it varies with the size needed), petrol, packing boxes or crates and insurance.

Services

There are a number of service charges to bear in mind:

- Electricity – there may be charges for tests or for installing new circuits or additional equipment in your new home.
- Gas – check if there are any disconnection or reconnection fees.
- Redirection of post – for each surname it costs £6.30 for one month, £13.65 for three months, £21 for six months and £31.50 for one year.
- Telephone – there is no connection charge if the line is simply swapped between old and new owners, but you will have to pay if the line is disconnected even if only for a few hours.

Ongoing vs one-off costs

All of the above are one-off costs which refer to the fees you are likely to face when buying a home, including moving in and making it habitable. They can range from a few hundred to many thousands of pounds. Ongoing costs refer to regular maintenance and bills, such as power and council tax or repairs.

Maintenance

Maintaining and repairing your own home can be expensive. Insurance – for both buildings and contents – is a necessity and costs each UK home-owner an average of £450 a year. But insurance doesn't cover everything and it is very easy to spend hundreds of pounds fixing a leaky roof or ancient boiler.

The best way to deal with the unexpected is to set up a contingency fund to help cushion the blow of any large repair or replacement bills.

Garden

If you are busy or simply not green-fingered, it would be a good idea to check the hourly rates of local gardeners. For about £6.50 an hour (more in central London), many will mow the lawn and keep the weeds down. A smart garden increases the value and appeal of a property; an unkempt and overgrown patch is an eyesore and would not make you very popular with the neighbours.

And if it all goes terribly wrong

Help from the State

Help with mortgage payments is available through the benefits system, but is limited:

- Income Support for Mortgage Interest (ISMI) will only be paid on a mortgage up to £100,000.
- Anyone taking out a loan after 1 October 1995 will not receive ISMI for the first nine months of a claim.
- Anyone whose loan was taken out before 2 October 1995 will not receive any support during the first two months of a claim and, during the following four months, only 50 per cent of the eligible mortgage interest will be paid.
- ISMI is paid by the DSS at a 'standard rate'. This may not match the rate charged by the lender on the borrower's mortgage account, which could lead to arrears. The Council of Mortgage Lenders has asked the Government to review how the standard rate is calculated to ensure that it is representative of rates charged across all lenders.
- ISMI will only pay the mortgage interest and not other outgoings, such as insurance premiums or a savings plan linked to a mortgage. In April 2001, the Government introduced two work incentive measures for homeowners receiving ISMI, namely 'mortgage interest run on' and a new '52-week linking rule'. Under mortgage interest run on, if borrowers come off benefit, they will continue to receive ISMI for a further four weeks. This is aimed at helping claimants back into work. The 52-week linking rule allows claimants to undertake short-term work without then having to wait a further nine months before being able to receive ISMI again.

Help from lenders for borrowers in difficulties

Most lenders will consider cases of financial difficulty and mortgage arrears sympathetically. The first step is to contact the mortgage company to discuss the matter.

With the borrower's co-operation, the lender will develop a plan for dealing with the financial difficulties and clearing the arrears. Most lenders seek to repossess a property only as a last resort.

What happens to a mortgage debt after a home is repossessed?

After a lender takes back a property, interest will generally continue to be charged on the mortgage loan until it is sold. There will also be other costs charged to the mortgage account, including estate agents' costs in selling the property and legal costs.

The lender has a legal duty to sell the property for the best price. If this results in a surplus after all the money owed to the lender and any other secured lender has been repaid, then this surplus is returned to the former borrower. But if the sale proceeds are not enough to pay off the money owing to the lender, the borrower faces a 'shortfall debt', which they still owe to the lender after possession.

What will the lender do if there is a shortfall debt?

The action taken depends on the circumstances. Usually, the lender will contact the borrower as soon as possible after the sale of the property and give a final financial statement. This will show the level of debt still owing to the lender.

If there is a shortfall debt, the lender may:

- immediately discuss proposals with the borrower on how they might repay the debt; or
- try to give the borrower some time to get back on their feet financially before contacting them about repaying the debt.

How long after the repossession can lenders seek the recovery of the debt?

In England, Wales and Northern Ireland, a lender legally has 12 years in which to contact the borrower to begin the process of obtaining repayment of shortfall debt; this period is usually five years in Scotland.

However, most lenders are committed to fair and sympathetic treatment of people who have suffered repossession and accept that individuals should not face long delays before lenders contact them to discuss repayment of the shortfall. Where a forwarding address is known, most lenders will contact borrowers fairly soon after possession, with a view to agreeing a manageable arrangement for repaying all or some of the debt.

In addition, from 11 February 2000, lenders who are members of the Council of Mortgage Lenders agreed that they will begin all recovery action for the shortfall within the first six years following the sale of a property in possession. Anyone whose property was taken into possession and sold more than six years ago, and who has not been contacted by their lender about recovering any outstanding debt will not now be asked to pay the shortfall.

Does this time limit apply to every case?

The new time limit does *not* affect anyone who is already:

- adhering to alternative payment arrangements for the shortfall debt; or
- who has already been contacted by the lender, even if the initial contact was made with them by the lender after six years from the date of the sale of the property in possession.

The six-year limit only refers to *beginning* recovery action and does not affect a lender's ability to recover the shortfall debt over a longer period. If there is evidence of mortgage fraud, the new time limit will not apply.

Following the sale of a property in possession, lenders often find it difficult to contact the former borrower. They use a variety of measures to identify where the individual is now living, including using tracing agents. Situations can arise where a lender or its third-party agent is trying to contact the individual (for example, by letter or telephone) to discuss repayment of the shortfall, but the individual simply chooses to *ignore* such contact – despite the fact that the contact is being made at the individual's new address. In these cases, lenders will consider that contact has been made for the purposes of the new six-year limit. If an individual is unclear about whether contact has been made within the six-year period, the lender will be able to confirm the position.

Inheritance tax

Inheritance tax is charged at 40 per cent on estates worth more than £250,000. Latest figures from the Halifax, the country's largest mortgage lender, estimates that the average semi-detached property in London is now worth roughly this amount. The average detached home is nudging £400,000. At this level, inheritance tax would be payable at 40 per cent on the difference between £250,000 and £400,000, which works out at £60,000. Recently, prices in the capital have been increasing at an average of 16 per cent a year, potentially adding more than £25,500 a year to the tax bill. At this rate, inheritance bills for the owner of a detached home in London or the South East could be going up by £500 a week.

Leading financial experts are calling on the Government to reform inheritance tax, arguing that it is unjust. The tax is studiously and easily avoided by the wealthy, and accountants often describe it as a voluntary tax for the rich. Princess Margaret, for example, is thought likely to have given away millions to her children to avoid inheritance tax, even though she still left an estate worth £7.6 million.

The Queen Mother's estate was passed on free of tax through a special concession, although it is thought that she had also put large chunks of money into trust for her grandchildren to ensure that there would be no bills.

But if your main asset is your home, you cannot easily use the devices available to the better off. Tax experts have warned that inheritance tax is a timebomb for homeowners, but appeals to Chancellor Gordon Brown to deal with the issue in his Budget yielded no change.

Inheritance tax, in one form or another, dates back to Roman times but in its modern form it was established in 1894 as estate duty under a Liberal government. The aim was to tax, and redistribute, inherited wealth. In 1975, under Labour Chancellor Dennis Healey, capital transfer tax was set up, with rates at up to a massive 75 per cent on inherited wealth. Capital transfer tax was replaced by the lower inheritance tax under the Conservative government in 1986.

Vulnerable people may be forced to raise mortgages or sell family homes to settle bills. In one case, a widower died, leaving his son, who had been living with him, a £400,000 house. This was the main asset and the son faced an inheritance tax bill of between £60,000 and £80,000. This could only be paid if he took on a mortgage or sold the family home.

One of the most effective ways to reduce inheritance tax liabilities is by gradually giving away assets before death. In families where the main asset is a home, options to reduce liability are limited. Property can pass between husbands and wives free of inheritance tax, so parents could each write wills leaving up to £250,000 to children and the remainder to each other, but this may effectively deprive a spouse of a property or income they need to live on.

Inheritance tax yields about £2.5 billion a year for the Government and to abolish it would cost the equivalent of one penny on income tax. Rather than scrap it, the Government could restructure it. Options include a significant increase in the £250,000 nil-rate band, exempting an individual's home and charging the tax on a sliding scale, rather than the 40 per cent that bites on every £1 over £250,000. Or maybe a capital gains tax on profits from assets at death would be more appropriate. Most homes would escape under rules allowing for a tapered reduction to zero in capital gains tax over a long period.

Many people do manage to avoid inheritance tax, however, either through good planning or through leaving assets to their spouse (which means it is not payable).

Below are some common questions:

What if I leave everything to my husband or wife?
No inheritance tax is payable, but you must both be domiciled in the UK.

What's the inheritance tax threshold?
This is £242,000 and, if you are liable for the tax, it will be levied at 40 per cent. The sum up to £242,000 is known as the nil-rate band.

What deductions are made?
Bequests to a spouse and UK charities are exempt, and outstanding bills, together with funeral costs, will also be deducted from the inheritance tax amount outstanding.

Who pays the tax office?
This will be paid by personal representatives – typically, any children. In some cases, children or heirs can find themselves having to pay the tax bill out of their own funds. Some people find themselves forced to take out bridging loans to meet tax liabilities because they are in the process of disposing of assets, which is why planning before you die can be very helpful.

When is money owed for inheritance tax payable?
It needs to be paid six months after the end of the month when the person has died. The authority to release the money held in the estate is known as probate in England and Wales and confirmation in Scotland.

How can I avoid paying inheritance tax through gifts?
The crucial issue with making gifts to below the inheritance threshold is that they are made seven years before you die – it is, in a sense, a clock ticking when you can beat the tax office.

What are the rules concerning gifts?
Although gifts made in the seven years before your death can be subject to inheritance tax, a number are exempt. A list of these can be found in *An Introduction to Inheritance Tax*, a leaflet available from the Inland Revenue. These gifts include: sums of money of up to £5,000 given as wedding gifts to children; maintenance payments to ex-partners and children; and other gifts of up to £3,000 made during a tax year.

Everyone has this £3,000 limit and, if it's not used up in one year, the amount can be carried forward to the next. After three years, the tax payable on a gift starts reducing until it reaches nil at year seven. Small gifts of up to £250 can be made to any number of people. This is known as taper relief.

The situation concerning gifts can be complicated and, again, it is an area where many people will want to seek advice from an experienced financial adviser.

What are 'potentially exempt transfers'?
It is just another term used for gifts made within the seven-year period to friends and relatives. If you die within the seven years, the value is added to your estate; if you don't, then the gift is exempt. You do not have to tell the tax office about gifts you have made, but the recipient is required to report the gift within a year of the donor's death.

If the death is within three years, 40 per cent is charged; after this, a sliding scale is applied. This is equivalent to a reduction of a fifth if the gift was made between three and four years before your death; another fifth if between four and five years; and so on, until the seventh year.

What are chargeable transfers?
Although there is no inheritance tax charged on a gift made seven years before you die, chargeable transfers can incur tax. These are sums of money transferred typically to trusts for which tax, payable at 20 per cent, is normally levied on the excess above £234,000.

These can also be known as discretionary trusts, which are administered by trustees and where the individual may have no immediate right to income. Gifts to companies are also known as chargeable transfers.

What about giving away a property?
Giving away your home to children or relatives will not mean you are automatically exempt from inheritance tax. If you plan to keep living in it, you need to prove you are paying the new landlord the correct market rent. The landlord could also face a capital gain tax bill when the property is sold, and the inheritance tax sum owed if you die within seven years of making the gift.

What about insurance policies?
Many people have life insurance and if you die and the proceeds are paid into your estate, this money could be subject to inheritance tax if it exceeds the £234,000 limit. The way around this is to have the policy

within a trust. Pension fund proceeds passed on to a spouse will also be free of tax.

What about gifts to charity?
Anything left to a UK charity is free of inheritance tax and this also applies to political parties and housing associations.

What about a trust to avoid inheritance tax?
Trusts are a good way of avoiding or paying less inheritance tax and a financial adviser can assist with setting these up. They are not necessarily a total escape from tax though – dependants may still face a tax bill, although at a far lower rate than 20 per cent.

Financial products are held within trusts and are typically provided by insurance companies. It is worth noting that some have higher charges than others. You will need advice on how to set these up. If you do not set up a trust, although you can transfer assets to a spouse tax-free, when they die and pass on wealth to the next generation, inheritance tax will be payable on everything beyond their £234,000 limit.

Life insurance can be written in trust. This applies mainly to whole of life policies. In the case of married couples, for example, a policy would be written on both lives, which pays a death benefit on the second death – when inheritance tax would arise.

You can also buy a policy called a 'gift inter vivos' – meaning a gift between two living people – which is also written within a trust. This is a temporary type of cover, aimed at meeting an inheritance tax liable if you die within seven years of making a lifetime gift. The death benefit will reduce as the potential tax liability reduces.

4
Legal and conveyancing – and buying at auction

Red tape

Conveyancing is the drawing up and checking of the legal contracts and records needed to transfer ownership of property from one person to another.

Typically the process takes about three months, with documentation sent by Royal Mail or Document Exchange, a private postal system used by solicitors. Homebuying in the UK takes twice as long as in most other European countries. According to the Land Registry, the longer conveyancing takes, the more likely the deal is to collapse through 'gazumping', 'gazundering' or the frustration of parties linked in the house-buying chain.

Remember, your solicitor works for you. Unlike the estate agent, whose main responsibility lies with the seller.

The first step is the solicitor acting on behalf of the seller requesting the title deeds – usually from the seller's mortgage company – and copies of the register and title plan from the Land Registry. The solicitor can then draw up the contract, which is sent to the buyer's solicitor, along with any other documents, such as replies to general inquiries.

The buyer's solicitor examines the contract and raises any questions. He conducts searches to ensure there are no plans for building nearby, and there is no contaminated land or old mines that could affect the property. He also checks over any lease. He also receives a copy of the buyer's mortgage offer, usually with instructions to act on behalf of the lender.

Once both parties have discussed the searches, answered questions and are satisfied, they sign identical copies of the sale contract, and the buyer's solicitor sends his or her client's contract and deposit to the seller's solicitor. Exchange takes place when the seller's solicitor sends the seller's contract to the buyer.

After this there are more contracts and documents to prepare, mortgage advances and settlement figures requested and transfers to be made before completion, when keys are handed over.

How do I choose my conveyancer?

Recommendation is often a good way to select a service provider such as a conveyancer. Some people prefer to use the family solicitor, while others prefer to go to a licensed conveyancer who deals solely with property matters. Obtaining a few quotes from different solicitors and licensed conveyancers will enable you to compare their prices and services.

You should take several things into consideration when choosing a conveyancer:

- While cost will obviously be a major factor, you should consider what kind of service you will be paying for. Ask for a breakdown of what the fee includes.
- Find out when your conveyancer can be contacted and how.
- Location may also be a factor. If you are relocating out of your area, you will have to decide whether to employ a conveyancer in the area that you are in currently or the area that you are moving to.

How can I speed up the process?

Once you are certain you will be moving and have decided on a conveyancer, there are several things you can do in anticipation of the move that can help to speed up the process.

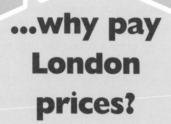

MOVING HOME – IS IT REALLY WORTH IT?

One hears so many horror stories about the difficulty of finding a good conveyancer to smooth your way into a new home that one asks the question: "is it really worth it?"

The answer to that question is a resounding "yes". Not only can you enjoy the new home for its surroundings, its facilities and its neighbourhood but there remains no better investment that you can possibly make than bricks and mortar. Buying and selling property is a way of life in this country and an important keystone of the British economy. Although it takes longer to negotiate the conveyancing process in this country than anywhere else in the world, we probably have one of the most active property markets in the world. The kind of property that we each live in reflects our financial circumstances from time to time and also reflects our personal circumstances, such as moving in to the correct neighbourhood to get the best schooling for our children or retiring to the countryside or the seaside once our day's work is done.

It may well be that the Government's much-heralded e-conveyancing will change the painful process of buying and selling a home. Something needs to make the process far easier than at the current time and a paperless lawyer's office is about a big a revolution as you can impose on conveyancing as one can imagine. However, that revolution is yet to occur and, in the meantime, we must ask ourselves: "how can we help ourselves?"

The best way to make things easier when it comes to selling is to make sure that your existing property is fit to sell. Have you kept those guarantees for the new double-glazing or the conservatory that you had built? Can you produce the Building Regulations Consent for your conservatory or the Planning Permission for your extension? Have you observed, and are you aware of, the dos and don'ts in your Legal Title? Have you decided what you are going to leave and what you are going to take? By getting all of this sorted out in advance, not only will it help your conveyancer but it will also cut down the amount of time spent in asking these questions, obtaining copy documents that are currently missed and ironing-out any problems which tend to protract the process in between the finding of your new buyer and exchanging contracts with that buyer.

When your buyer is found, check him out just as thoroughly. Make sure your estate agent has gone into the detail of any associated chain of transactions. Can your buyer afford the mortgage he will require to buy the property? Ask the searching questions at the beginning of the transaction and not half-way through it.

Similar early preparation on the property you are buying will equally help. Can you afford the mortgage you will require? Has it been agreed in principle? Organise your survey as quickly as possible after your offer has been accepted. Do you have any particular questions you want your lawyer to ask on the property you are buying? If so, tell him at the outset what those points of concern are.

The process of buying and selling is the interaction of a very large number of individuals and organisations. To some extent, the efficiency with which they all communicate with one another depends on the amount of energy your conveyancer puts into it. Equally however, it is important for you to help yourself and to work with your conveyancer by getting as much of the practical groundwork out of the way early on as you possibly can.

One final point. There is a huge difference between buying a leasehold property and a freehold property. The formalities with regard to a leasehold acquisition are more searching, more detailed and take much longer. Legal fees on a leasehold sale or purchase are likely to be greater. If you are concerned about speed and, for that matter, if you are looking for a better capital investment, a basic rule of thumb is to go for a freehold rather than a leasehold if you can possibly afford it. It is generally a better bet all the way round.

Your buyer's conveyancer (or your conveyancer for the property if you are buying) will have to undertake searches on the property. If you are selling, your conveyancer may need to get your title deeds to provide a plan of the property, so it is worth getting your conveyancer to request the deeds from your lender or solicitor (if different from the conveyancer) as early as possible.

Depending on the local authority and the amount of work needed to be done, searches can be time-consuming, so the sooner they are made the better.

In the same way as hold ups in any one of these things can cause cumulative delays, dealing with them as early as possible could help to speed up the process.

Your conveyancer may even draw up a draft contract in advance that can be adjusted to fit the details of the specific purchase. This can be done at a very early stage and can also help to avoid delays.

E-conveyancing

The Land Registry, the official body that records who owns what land in England and Wales, believes that by moving the system online, it will become faster and more transparent and reduce the risk of deals falling through. The e-conveyancing system it has proposed will enable authorised solicitors, licensed conveyancers, estate agents, mortgage lenders and other professionals connected with the buying and selling process to conduct business with each other and with the registry using a private, secure, nationwide network. They would have electronic access to the information needed to carry out all stages of the conveyancing process online, including the electronic transfer of money.

In theory, this should enable solicitors to spot and solve problems as soon as they crop up. But the consultation paper asks whether information – not only about their own sale but also about others in their chain – should be made directly available to the public. However, until a majority of the UK population has access to the Internet, solicitors could

Simple Conveyancing:

1. Click for a Quote

2. Instruct us

3. Put the kettle on!

Whether you're buying, selling or remortgaging a property, Online Conveyancing makes it as easy as **1**, **2**, **3**.

1. **An instant quote is just a click away** – key in your house price for an online quote in seconds.

2. **Instruct us** – complete one simple form to start the ball rolling.

3. **Web tracker** – access your own secure page 24 hours a day for up-to-date progress on your conveyancing.

Just click onto our website below, or call us on **01244 408300** or email us at enquiries@onlineconveyancing.co.uk.

www.onlineconveyancing.co.uk

ONLINE CONVEYANCING is an internet specialist division of Drummonds Solicitors
Windsor House, Pepper Street, Chester CH1 1DF

Take Some of the Stress out of Moving or Remortgaging – Instruct Your Solicitor Online

Instructing a solicitor to act for you in connection with your house sale or purchase has never been easier. **Drummonds solicitors** is an experienced solicitors practice based in Chester which provides conveyancing and remortgaging services to clients throughout England and Wales.

Drummonds is a modern forward-thinking solicitors practice which has invested in the latest technology to enable it to provide an even better service to clients.

Drummonds solicitors was established in 1991 and has been providing online conveyancing services to clients for over 2 years through its dedicated website:

www.onlineconveyancing.co.uk

Prospective buyers or sellers initially go direct to the site to obtain a **competitive quotation** for their conveyancing or remortgaging needs. The quotation details all likely charges in connection with the sale, purchase or remortgage. Online conveyancing operates on a **no move – no legal fee** basis although disbursements incurred, such as search fees do have to be paid for.

If you are happy with the online quotation you can then instruct Drummonds online and inform your estate agent that **Drummonds Online Conveyancing** will be acting for you.

You will be reassured that **professionally qualified solicitors**, regulated by the Law Society, but working with their teams will be acting for you in your house move.

Once **Drummonds Online Conveyancing** has been instructed you are given a personal password with access to a **webtracker** page. This allows you to follow the progress of your move just by logging onto the website from your own computer either at home or in the workplace at any time of day or night.

The Drummonds Online webtracker is updated throughout each working day.

As an alternative **SMS updates** can be provided or you may contact your solicitor and the team looking after you at Online Conveyancing by **email**.

When dealing with your purchase your solicitor will carry out a full investigation of the title to the property and will prepare a detailed user-friendly property report for you. This will be sent with the legal documents that need to be signed by you such as the mortgage deed and the contract all together in one envelope. The report can be studied in the comfort of your own home or work-place. There is no necessity to attend a time-consuming meeting at the solicitors office.

The www.onlineconveyancing.co.uk website also contains lots of useful information including **guides to buying and selling property** and a helpful **jargon buster**. It is well worth a look just for this.

If you are looking to **Remortgage** your property Online Conveyancing will be able to help. Again a competitive quotation can be obtained direct from the website and a similar webtracking service is available.

Overall **Drummonds Online Conveyancing** provides a modern efficient approach to conveyancing and remortgaging. This is combined with the knowledge that there is always a professional and reassuringly friendly voice at the end of the telephone when needed from your solicitor and their supporting team.

For more information log onto:
www.onlineconveyancing.co.uk

reasonably argue that communication with clients should still be conducted by post.

The proposed system does not include local councils, and, as anyone who has bought a house knows, obtaining a local search can take many weeks. However, the registry points out that the Government plans to introduce Sellers' Packs by 2006, which means the seller will have to sort out searches before the property is even put on the market.

The new system is not likely to be introduced before 2006. To find out more about the proposals and to have your say about the current system and how you think it can be improved, visit the Land Registry's website (www.landreg.gov.uk).

Auctions

Properties are sold at auctions if they have been repossessed by mortgage lenders, housing associations or councils, or need large-scale work that will deter buyers going through conventional estate agents.

If you are buying, prepare in advance. Most auctions are in hotels and are advertised by participating estate agents and valuers. Contact them for a catalogue of properties under the hammer at the next auction (often this is done via a premium rate telephone line, costing about £5 a call).

The catalogue will contain photos of the properties, details of tenure – mostly 'full vacant possession', meaning no chain – and guide prices, which are normally the minimum the sellers will accept.

If you like the look of a property, visit it well before sale day. Auctioneers arrange group viewings for all potential buyers or ask local estate agents to do individual viewings.

About 15 per cent of properties in catalogues are sold before the auction because a keen buyer has made a deal with the seller, so if you see a property you like in the catalogue, try making an advance bid through the auction house. You have nothing to lose.

Some sellers and their estate agents have 'pre-sale surveys' and will give you details. These are often reliable but most mortgage lenders want an independent survey, and you will have to pay for this – despite running the risk of being outbidded for the property.

Ahead of the auction, arrange a solicitor and mortgage lender as in a conventional house purchase. Ensure you have funds covering the likely sale price (experts suggest the guide price plus 15 per cent to be safe), plus solicitors' fees, moving costs and repair work. You must pay 10 per cent of the property's cost at the auction if your bid is successful.

At the auction each property is called a 'lot'. When your preferred lot comes up, the auctioneer will confirm the address and details before asking for bids. The bids usually rise in £5,000 levels until they approach the guide price, when bids will rise in £2,000 or £1,000 sums. Stay cool and remain well within your budget, or even get a friend to bid on your behalf if you are nervous.

If you are successful, you pay 10 per cent of the cost immediately and the rest within 28 days. Remember – once the hammer has come down, neither the buyer nor the seller can withdraw.

Forthcoming auctions are listed at www.eigroup.co.uk and www.propertyauctions.com.

5

Mortgages

How much can I borrow?

The amount you can borrow depends mainly on your income. You need to find out roughly how much you might be able to borrow before you go house hunting. That way, you know the price range you can afford.

The traditional approach

Lenders generally take the view that buyers can afford about three times their annual pre-tax income, sometimes slightly more. For couples who are both working, the 'income multiple' is generally three times the larger salary, plus one times the second.

Quite a few lenders will be prepared to consider a higher income-to-loan multiple. There are companies out there who offer 100 per cent mortgages and you may find this tempting, but before you opt to borrow more, work out whether you can actually afford it.

Going for a bigger loan

Some lenders will lend on the basis of affordability rather than income multiples. They look at your monthly income and outgoings, and base the amount they are prepared to lend on your individual circumstances. This approach can come up with a much bigger loan than you would normally be offered using traditional income multiples. Do your budgeting carefully if you take up such an offer.

A CHEAPER
MORTGAGE AT 3.8%

FLEXIBLE OFFSET MORTGAGE

3.35% | 4.9%

DISCOUNTED RATE FOR 3 MONTHS | APR VARIABLE

THAT'S WHAT OFFSETTING
MEANS TO ME

That's the beauty of an Intelligent Finance mortgage. Not only do you get great flexible benefits, you can also offset the money you have with them against your mortgage to make your money work harder. So how does offsetting work for me? I have £8,000 in my savings and current account and a 25 year, £95,000 mortgage with Intelligent Finance. Instead of receiving interest on my savings and current account, I'll pay NO interest on £8,000 of my mortgage. If I leave things as they are, I could reduce the total amount I'll pay on my mortgage by a staggering £16,369 and pay it off earlier.

If I didn't have any money to offset against my mortgage, assuming all other circumstances are the same, I'd have to find an incredibly low interest rate of 3.8% for 25 years to match the total amount I'd pay by offsetting. That's why, for me, offsetting means a cheaper mortgage. **For an intelligent mortgage visit our website or give us a call.**

INTELLIGENT FINANCE™
the way all banks will be

0845 606 4343
www.if.com
or contact your Financial Adviser

INTELLIGENT FINANCE offset banking from the **HALIFAX**

How Intelligent Finance could make the most of your money

Intelligent Finance can offer you a mortgage, savings, personal loan, current account and credit card. Like all good ideas, ours is very simple. We offset the money you have in your current account and/or savings against the money you borrow from us, such as a credit card, personal loan or mortgage for interest calculations.

This means that, while you don't earn interest on the money you have with us, you pay no interest on the equivalent balance of your borrowings. So, for example, if you had a 25-year mortgage of £95,000 and savings of £8,000 with us, you would pay no interest on £8,000 of the mortgage. If you leave things as they are, you could reduce the total amount you'll pay on your mortgage by a staggering £16,369 and pay it off earlier.

Online Banking made easier

Banking on-line may seem frightening but could benefit many bank customers. You can log onto the internet at any time (day or night) and phone lines are open long after bank branches have locked up for the night. It also means the end of spending lunchtimes queuing at your local bank branch.

Intelligent Finance gives you constant, instant access to your finances and enables you to manage your own financial affairs more closely than ever. Imagine planning a night out with friends and being able to log on or call to find out if you'll be able to paint the town red – or just a slight tinge of pink. You can also check balances as often as you like to find out if cheques have cleared, direct debits paid, and more.

With the click of a mouse, you can transfer funds, set up or amend direct debits and standing orders, pay bills or even apply for new products on-line. Intelligent Finance gives customers decisions, in principle, within minutes of applying on-line.

Keeping your payments down

Generally speaking, you should try not to pay more than 40 per cent of your net (take home) pay in mortgage payments. This is just a guideline: in London, for example, you may well find half your income going on the mortgage.

On top of that there are the ongoing costs of owning a house: council tax, utilities and maintenance. It's hard to estimate costs before you move in, but overall you should try to keep the total cost of your home to a maximum of 60 per cent of your monthly take-home pay.

The valuation limit

Most people borrow only 95 per cent of the property's valuation, which can be lower than the price you have agreed with the seller. Many lenders give better deals to people with large deposits, so it can make sense to dip into savings, as the smaller the deposit, the higher the interest rate you may have to pay.

You can get 100 per cent mortgages, but the rates are generally uncompetitive and you will pay above the odds to borrow at this level. It is much better to save for a deposit.

The size of your mortgage compared to the value of your property is called the loan to value (LTV) ratio – a £90,000 mortgage on a £100,000 home gives a LTV of 90 per cent. The Council of Mortgage Lenders says the average first-time buyer's mortgage is 74 per cent LTV, and their average mortgage is £86,000. Other buyers have an average 62 per cent LTV ratio with a £93,000 mortgage.

Finding the right mortgage for you

Mortgages come in a wide and confusing variety, but if you choose carefully you should be able to get a mortgage that suits you. You need to decide first on the type of loan you want, then think about which approach to repaying your loan is best for you.

What other building society can help you with mortgages, removals and free gazumping insurance?

- At Britannia, we've put together a unique package to help steer you through the murky waters of home buying.

- For a start, our mortgages have appeared in national newspapers' 'Best Buy' tables, every month, for over three years.

- We can give you a helping tentacle to move house, with a removals service guaranteed to be available on the day you want to move.

- And on top of all that, Britannia is the only building society to offer free gazumping insurance. Covering lost legal and valuation fees if you get gazumped or your purchase falls through.

- So whatever happens no one's going to make a sucker out of you.

- Telephone us on **0845 840 0077** or visit our website **www.britannia.co.uk/buying**

mutual Britannia

Britannia in a word, your home for life

The following is a brief summary of the main types of loan available:

- **Variable rate:** the standard mortgage product, and often the most expensive of the range available. Rates move up and down more or less in line with the Bank of England base rate, but at the lender's discretion and at a level typically 1.75 per cent higher than base rate.
- **Tracker rate:** the rate is guaranteed to move in line with the Bank of England base rate by a set amount and usually for a set period, although in some cases the guarantee is for the life of the mortgage.
- **Discounted rate:** you get a discount on the standard variable rate, or the tracker rate, for a set period. This is often set in steps, with the discount decreasing in stages over a year or more.
- **Fixed rate:** the rate you pay is fixed for a set period, typically between one and five years. Your monthly payments therefore stay the same during that period, regardless of what happens to interest rates. However, beware of any redemption penalties that might tie you in to the lender's variable rate after the fixed period has ended.
- **Capped rate:** the rate cannot go above a specified upper limit, but will follow rates down if they fall. Like fixed rates, these are normally for a set period, between one and five years.
- **Cashback:** you get a cash payment when the loan is finalised, generally as a percentage of the loan amount, eg three per cent. You usually have to pay the standard variable rate for a fixed period, or pay back some of the cash if you want to get out of the deal early.
- **CAT standard:** the loan meets standards laid down by the Government for costs, access and terms. These ensure that you pay a fair rate of interest and there are no hidden charges or unfair terms in the small print.
- **Flexible:** this is really a repayment option rather than a type of loan. It helps you to pay off your mortgage earlier without penalty and cut your interest costs.

How do you want to repay your mortgage?

It is worth thinking about your mortgage loan even before you hit the high street or search the Internet. There are only two main ways to pay off the mortgage, but they are very different in the way they work and the effect they have on your debt.

Debt is an expensive luxury, especially when inflation is low and there are no tax breaks on debt interest. Aim to pay off your mortgage as quickly as possible – it is the most effective form of saving there is. You can do that by choosing a shorter repayment term than the usual 25 years, for example.

Repayment mortgage

A repayment mortgage is guaranteed to pay off your mortgage by the end of the term. That makes it the safest way to repay your loan. It works just like a normal personal loan – each month, you pay back some of the original capital plus interest on the outstanding balance.

In the early years, most of your repayments are made up of interest, with the result that you only pay off a small proportion of the capital. But you can pay in extra lump sums, or overpay regularly, to reduce your debt and cut the amount of interest you have to pay. Redemption penalties on some special deals may prevent you doing this, though, so check first.

Most mortgages are paid back over a period of 25 years, but you can opt for a shorter repayment period if you can afford the higher payments. Depending on your age, you may also have to accept a shorter period.

Repayment mortgages are good if you prefer the safety-first approach and want to be sure you will eventually pay off your mortgage.

Interest-only mortgage

If you opt for an interest-only mortgage, your monthly payments will seem much cheaper than those for a comparable repayment loan. But that's because you are only paying back interest – it's up to you to come up with the cash to repay the original loan amount at the end of the mortgage term (usually 20 or 25 years).

Most people decide to set up an investment plan to pay off the capital they owe. This can be stock market-based (using an individual savings account (ISA), for example) or through an endowment policy. These are no longer very popular as they tend to be inflexible and expensive.

All mortgage-linked savings schemes should aim to grow at a rate higher than the amount you are paying in interest. If they fail to achieve this, they will not provide enough money to pay off your mortgage.

A few people don't take out investments but rely on house price rises to pay off their loan when they sell up. This can be risky if you don't have much of a deposit to put down on a property – and if prices drop instead of going up.

You can make capital repayments with an interest only mortgage to reduce your mortgage debt faster and cut interest payments, just as you can with a repayment mortgage. But check there are no redemption penalties first.

Interest-only mortgages are good if:

- you expect investment returns (after charges) to be higher than mortgage rates;
- you expect to earn bonuses that you can use to pay down your mortgage regularly, or inherit money that you can use to pay off your mortgage;
- you expect house prices to rise substantially so that you have enough equity in your property to pay off your loan.

They are not so good if you don't want to take the risk that your investment will not grow fast enough to pay off the mortgage.

Flexible and current account/offset mortgages

Flexible mortgages are repayment mortgages that enable you to pay off your mortgage earlier and cut your interest costs. They offer the ability to

INTRODUCING OFFSET ACCOUNTS

Making your money work harder

'Bundled mortgages', 'current account mortgages' or 'combination products' – just some of the names given to the increasingly popular offset mortgage or account.

Whilst lenders may name and operate their offset accounts differently, the basic principle is the same – they combine your savings with your borrowings to make your money work harder.

The simplest offset account uses savings to reduce your outstanding mortgage balance. Rather than earning interest on your savings, every pound in your savings account reduces the interest charged on your mortgage. Generally, interest charged on your borrowings is more than the interest you receive on your savings, so reducing the mortgage balance by any amount will make you better off.

Many people believe that a large lump sum is needed to make an offset account worthwhile but you don't need a lot of savings to make it work. An offset account can mean huge savings to any borrower who puts away even a small amount. The table shows how by saving the price of your lunch every day, or just £1 per day, you could save thousands of pounds in interest charges and build a sizeable nest egg. And of course the savings balance isn't tied to the mortgage, so if a rainy day comes along, you have access to your money.

	Saving per month	Interest payments saved	Mortgage paid off	Savings nest egg built
Cost of lunch every day	£130	£24,823	4 years and 6 months early	£31,980
£1 a day	£30	£8,550	18 months early	£8,460

You pay less tax

Most of us like paying less tax and one of the big advantages of an offset account is that because you don't receive interest on your savings, the taxman can't tax you on them. David Heshon, Product Development Manager at Yorkshire Building Society said " the tax benefit of offset accounts is clearly an advantage to everyone, but to higher rate taxpayers the money saved can be significant."

The equivalent savings rate which can be available from offset accounts is generally far higher than can be accessed through conventional savings accounts – including other tax free savings such as Individual Savings Accounts (ISAs). Even in today's low interest rate environment the equivalent of more than 7% gross return is achievable for higher rate taxpayers.

Flexible to your needs

Offset accounts can be financially beneficial to almost any borrower, but another great advantage is flexibility. For borrowers wanting to overpay, underpay or take a payment holiday, offsetting can help. A standard flexible mortgage would require that you build up 'credit' by overpaying, before these options were available, but by offsetting your savings against your mortgage and keeping the same monthly payment you will naturally be over-paying your mortgage.

The Future's Offset

Not surprisingly, offset accounts and current account mortgages are increasingly popular with all types of people – a trend likely to continue due to the above benefits.

Whatever your lifestyle a Current Account Mortgage could offer something to suit everyone!

Once again we have found the mortgage market taking a new direction with many borrowers now opting for a Current Account Mortgage.

So why the shift?

Many customers are looking for a mortgage that will offer them the flexibility they need throughout all the various life stages without having the hassle of having to switch mortgages as their circumstances change.

A Current Account Mortgage does this in that it offers flexible features to match the changing needs of most individuals. You can usually tailor a Current Account Mortgage to suit your current needs.

So how does this work in reality?

Take for example James, a young sole-occupant living in his first home. He has no major additional expenditure other than his house so has left substantially more money in his Current Account Mortgage over the last few years than he needed to. A couple of years later wedding bells ring and James has to find the funds to finance this expensive event. However, this is no problem as having a Current Account Mortgage means that he can now leave less of his salary in the account each month in order to free up cash for the big day subject to him remaining within any limits that apply.

James and his new wife Sarah then continue to leave their surplus monthly income in their account until a few years later when they are overjoyed with the news that they are expecting their first child. Whilst this may create a financial headache for most people it is not a problem in this case. Why? Well they have a Current Account Mortgage. They can now take a repayment holiday allowing one of them the ability to finish work for a while to care for the new arrival subject to the terms and conditions applied by their mortgage lender.

There may be many occasions when additional major expense is required, a new car for example, home improvements, school fees and other expensive items. With the Current Account Mortgage Equity Release facility this is not a problem as James and Sarah will have access to some of the equity they have built up in their home subject to the terms and conditions applied by their mortgage lender and any limits that apply. Access to the funds is easy too as most Current Account Mortgages come with a cheque book, a card for cheque guarantee, Switch and ATM functionality, Telephone Banking and Internet Banking in addition to regular statements to help them budget. What's more, any money they withdraw will be at their Current Account Mortgage Rate which may be lower than that charged on a conventional Personal Loan.

Eventually James and Sarah reach a stage in their life when the kids leave home and they find they have more disposable income which they leave in their Current Account Mortgage. By leaving these funds in their Current Account Mortgage they could save time and money on their mortgage when compared to a standard mortgage with interest calculated annually. How does this work I hear you ask? Well, on most Current Account Mortgages interest is calculated daily. Because interest is calculated on a daily basis, every day makes a difference to the amount they eventually save. But it's not like they've used their savings to repay their mortgage. The money simply sits in their account, warding off interest from their mortgage. Each time either their salary or a portion of savings is posted into the account, these will immediately reduce the outstanding mortgage balance and consequently the amount on which they are paying interest.

What does this mean for you? Well it means you could retire early to enjoy the good life! Just like James and Sarah!

One Current Account Mortgage which offers all of the above is the Yorkshire Bank Rapid Repay Account. For more information on this or Yorkshire Bank's full range of mortgage products either call **0800 20 21 22*** or contact any Yorkshire Bank Branch.

*For your security, Calls to the 0800 number may be monitored or recorded.

overpay, underpay, and take payment holidays. Any overpayments you make are immediately credited against what you owe. With traditional mortgages, overpayments are usually only credited once a year, and may not be possible at all if redemption penalties apply.

Flexible mortgages also charge interest on a daily or monthly basis, instead of the normal annual basis. This makes a big difference to the amount of interest you pay in total.

Most flexible loans are traditional mortgages with additional flexibility. These come in the usual variety, with discounted, fixed and tracker rates available.

Truly flexible loans are the relatively new type of current account or offset mortgage products. Both types allow you to put your mortgage, credit card, personal loan, current account and savings in one pot. This effectively means you earn tax-free interest on your savings as all your money is being used to offset your mortgage. And all your borrowing is also effectively at a lower rate of interest.

The main difference between the two types of account is that the current account product puts everything in one pot, producing one statement, while offset products keep your accounts separate.

Flexible loans are good if:

- you expect to be able to make overpayments, either regularly or occasionally;
- you have irregular earnings that make flexibility with mortgage payments important;
- you can benefit from the tax and interest advantages of having all your money in one pot. This generally applies to high earners and people with significant savings to offset their debts.

Flexible loans are not good if:

- you are unlikely to use the flexibility, need to budget or want to keep your mortgage costs as low as possible. Flexible loan rates are not usually the most competitive, and you may be better off with a discounted or fixed rate mortgage in these circumstances;

- you are undisciplined with money. Current account mortgages in particular are no good for spendthrifts who cannot mentally put aside an amount to pay the mortgage each month, when it does not physically disappear from their account.

Pension-linked mortgage

It's unusual to see these being sold today, although you may have a pension-linked mortgage if taken out a few years ago. Basically, you are expected to use the tax-free lump sum from a maturing pension to pay off your mortgage.

The attraction is that all payments into a personal pension attract generous Inland Revenue tax rebates. Review your repayment plan regularly to make sure it is still on track to pay off your mortgage. You may have to increase payments if growth is lower than expected.

Repaying an interest-only loan

At a time of soaring property prices many buyers choose an interest-only mortgage because the monthly repayments are cheaper. Some really live dangerously and put off setting up any investments to pay off the capital at the end of the term. But this isn't advisable unless you are very confident about your future finances.

The main ways people do pay off interest-only loans are outlined here.

ISAs

Saving cash in an individual savings account (ISA) is increasingly popular as a way to back up your mortgage. You'll need to pick up a fund investing in stocks and shares that are expected to grow fairly fast – if the ISAs do well, you could pay off the mortgage early.

You can put up to £7,000 into a stock market ISA each tax year, so a couple can make £14,000 worth of investments. The downside is that you will open yourself up to stock market fluctuations.

Endowments

Endowments are savings schemes with built-in life insurance, sold by insurance companies. The contract usually runs for 25 years, meaning you can't pay off the loan early.

With-profits endowments offer you an annual bonus, which can't be taken away, plus a further bonus when the policy matures. This can be worth up to 60 per cent of a policy's final value. Your cash is invested in a giant fund containing stocks and shares, property and fixed-interest investments.

Endowments have some well-publicised performance problems, so be very cautious if you are offered one. An ISA is easier and cheaper to run than an endowment, and a lot more flexible. Salespeople earn a lot of commission from selling endowments, so some firms still try the hard sell. Watch out.

How to find the best deal

Shop around

Small or obscure building societies and mortgage brokers often offer better rates than High Street banks and building societies.

Mutuality pays

Building societies generally offer a better mortgage deal than most banks, certainly on variable rates. And with some societies, there is the possibility of a demutualisation windfall if the society floats on the stockmarket or is taken over.

Look beyond the headline rate

The initial interest rate quoted in tables or adverts may be temptingly – but also temporarily – low. Find out what rate you will pay when the special deal finishes.

Check for redemption penalties

These are common on many types of mortgage, and make it expensive to switch out of a loan while they apply. They usually apply only for the term of a special deal, but they may extend beyond that term where the initial rate is particularly low, tying you into the lender's standard variable rate for several years. Loans like this with extended penalties are not usually good value.

Watch out for compulsory insurance

To qualify for some loans, you have to buy insurance from or through your lender – typically buildings or contents cover. You can invariably buy such cover more cheaply from another source. If you are considering such a deal, factor in additional interest of at least 0.25 per cent to reflect the price of an uncompetitive insurance policy.

Will you have to pay a MIG?

If you are borrowing more than 90 per cent of the value of your home you may be asked to pay a mortgage indemnity guarantee (MIG) – sometimes called a 'high lending fee'. This is a one-off payment that buys an insurance policy that will pay out if you get into mortgage arrears and the house is repossessed. But beware – this does nothing to protect you! Many lenders don't charge a MIG any more. If it's demanded from you, check whether you could get a better deal elsewhere.

How often is interest calculated?

Daily or monthly calculations work better than annual ones for borrowers who want to repay capital regularly. With annual interest any capital repayment made over a 12-month period is only credited once a year, on a lender's chosen anniversary. The interest you pay throughout the next 12 months relates to the sum owed at that earlier point. With daily or monthly interest, all capital repayments are credited as soon as they are made. This means that future interest you pay relates to the reduced sum still left outstanding. Because you owe less, you pay less interest.

Check minimum capital repayment to trigger a recalculation

Most lenders who calculate interest annually will do a recalculation if you pay in a big enough lump sum and ask for the calculation to be done. Find out what the minimum is – it may be just £100 or up to £1,000.

Take all costs into account

When comparing mortgage costs, be sure to include application, valuation, legal and other fees. If the rate varies over the term of any special deal, work out what rate you will pay on average and use that in comparisons.

Beware the stated APR (annual percentage rate)

Depending on many hidden factors, a loan with a low APR may be more expensive overall than one with a higher APR.

Getting advice

Advice on mortgages is offered by estate agents, mortgage brokers, financial advisers, and lenders – but there are no laws governing mortgage advice, so tread carefully.

What sort of advice will you get?

Lenders will only offer advice on their own products. Estate agents will generally deal with a few lenders with which they have a relationship. Some estate agents are subsidiaries of a lender, and only offer mortgages from that lender. If you want advice, mortgage brokers are a better bet, although they, too, may deal with a panel of lenders rather than covering the whole market.

If you use a mortgage broker, find out how you will be charged before you start discussions. Some brokers get paid entirely by commission from lenders, while others charge a fee, typically one per cent of the loan you take.

Follow the mortgage code

There are no laws governing quality or training standards for mortgage advisers, as there are for investment advisers. But most lenders and mortgage intermediaries follow a voluntary code of conduct, which includes guidelines for giving advice. The code says that brokers must tell you:

- whether they trawl the whole marketplace to find the most suitable mortgage or choose from a panel of selected lenders;
- whether they are acting as your representative or the lender's;
- whether they will receive a fee from the lender for putting mortgage business their way.

You can find out whether a mortgage broker subscribes to the mortgage code by asking for their registration number. Or check with the Mortgage Code Compliance Board to see if they are registered on the helpline number 01785 218200.

Can you save yourself money by remortgaging?

Remortgaging is what you do when you switch your mortgage to a new lender without actually buying a new home.

Why remortgage?

Like millions of borrowers, you probably have a variable rate mortgage. If you don't have a redemption penalty on your current loan, you could save many hundreds of pounds a year by switching to a better value fixed or discounted loan. For example, if you are paying 7.5 per cent on a standard variable rate, your monthly interest payments on a £100,000 interest-only loan work out at £625. Switch to a discounted rate where you pay 5.5 per cent for one year and your monthly payments immediately fall to £458, a saving of £2,000 over a year.

With savings like these to be made, it may be worth switching your loan even if you would have to pay a redemption penalty. You need to work out how much you will save compared with the penalty involved.

Are there any costs?

You may have to pay an application fee, a valuation fee and solicitors' fees too. That could add up to £700 or £800, which may wipe out any potential savings from a lower rate if you have a small loan.

Some lenders offer special deals for borrowers looking to remortgage to minimise these costs. The rate may not be the most competitive, but it is balanced by benefits such as a free valuation, no application fee, and cashback of £250 or £300 to cover your legal costs. This can work well if you have a small loan.

It is worth talking to your own lender before moving your mortgage to find out if they can offer you a better deal. You could avoid some of the costs involved in switching to a new lender.

Research the market

Take a good look around before deciding where to apply. You may get special remortgage terms from some lenders, but you will also be excluded from some deals that lenders do not make available to borrowers who want to remortgage. These are some of the points to watch:

- Look at the rate you will move on to after any special deal has ended, and think about whether it might mean having to remortgage again in a few years' time.

- Consider, instead, switching to a lender who offers good value over the longer term, perhaps by pledging to maintain a competitive standard variable rate.

- Take a look at flexible current account and offset mortgages to see if they would suit you. The tax advantages and cost efficiency of such schemes can be compelling.

Take a look at the earlier section on How to Find the Best Deal (see pages 62–64) to brush up on the pitfalls of the mortgage market.

Getting a mortgage if you are self-employed, work on contract or have an impaired credit record can be hard work. But now competition between lenders is so intense most obstacles can be overcome.

Hard-to-get mortgages

Self-employed

If you haven't been self-employed for very long, you will probably find it hard to get a loan until you have established yourself, unless you have gone into a business in which you are already experienced and can demonstrate a track record.

Lenders will generally want to see three years of accounts to prove your income before deciding whether to offer you a loan. But they are gradually getting more relaxed about this sector of the economy, and some lenders are happy with 12 months of accounts.

One common problem if you are self-employed is that your accounts are likely to understate the profits from your business, for perfectly legitimate reasons. That cuts down the amount you can borrow. One way around this is to opt for a self-certification loan, where you state what your income is, but do not have to prove it. This type of loan is generally more expensive than conventional loans, and has the added drawback that you may not be able to borrow as large a proportion of the property's value.

Contract workers

Contract workers may have to shop around to find a lender willing to take them on, or use a mortgage broker who will know which lenders to approach. Some lenders will want to see that your contract has been renewed regularly over a one or two year period. Others may be happy if your contract has been renewed at least once by the same employer.

Mortgage arrears

You may be turned down for a mortgage if you have fallen behind with your payments on a previous loan. Lenders conduct a credit search to discover your credit history, and often use a system of credit scoring to assess your creditworthiness. If you don't get enough points, you could be refused a loan, and mortgage arrears will obviously affect your score.

Many lenders will lend to people with a history of mortgage arrears, but only under certain conditions. They may limit the proportion of the property value they are prepared to lend, and specify a maximum number of months' arrears, typically three or six months. They may also refuse to consider your application if the arrears occurred within a specified time period, for example, within the last 12 months.

You may have to turn to specialist lenders if you cannot meet the conditions demanded by mainstream lenders. But that will generally mean having to pay a higher rate of interest. You can take a look at the conditions specified by lenders if you select the 'arrears' category of mortgages in the mortgage tables and click through to each lender's details.

County court judgements

County court judgements, or CCJs, are issued for unpaid debt. They stay on your credit reference file for six years from the date of the judgement, or until the debt is paid off.

If you cleared the debt more than a year ago, you stand a good chance of getting a mortgage from mainstream lenders. You are likely to find it harder if you paid it off more recently; and if it is still unpaid, you will generally be refused a mortgage by High Street lenders. Specialist lenders may offer you a loan, but on uncompetitive terms.

You can take a look at the conditions specified by lenders for CCJs if you select the CCJs category of mortgages in the mortgage tables and click through to each lenders' details.

Checking your credit history

If you want to check your own credit rating, send your name and address, together with a cheque or postal order for £2 and a list of your previous addresses over the last six years, to both of the following agencies:

Equifax
Credit File Advice Centre,
PO Box 3001,
Glasgow, G81 2DT.

Experian
Consumer Help Service,
PO Box 8000,
Nottingham, NG1 5GX.

First-time buyers

Getting 100 per cent

Several lenders offer 100 per cent mortgages, although not all make them available to first-time buyers. Scottish Widows even offer 110 per cent on its Professional Mortgage – a loan aimed at those in structured careers, who are likely to earn more as they get older.

There are a couple of problems with 100 per cent loans. First, there is the potential for negative equity. If the value of your property falls by 5 per cent and you have a 10 per cent stake in it, you still have 5 per cent equity in the property. If it falls by 5 per cent and you don't have equity in the property, you are in a negative equity position.

Few economists believe house prices will fall in the near future, but some lenders like the NatWest and Alliance & Leicester have decided to restrict 100 per cent deals in some areas.

Another problem with 100 per cent deals is they tend to attract higher rates than smaller mortgages. For instance, a borrower who puts down a 10 per cent deposit is only charged 5.99 per cent for two years (by one supermarket lender) but those who take a 100 per cent loan are charged 6.3 per cent. However, once you have built up 10 per cent equity in the property you can move to the lower rate.

Any cashback?

An alternative to a 100 per cent mortgage is a cashback deal. At Bristol & West you may be denied 100 per cent as a first-time buyer but you can borrow 95 per cent loan-to-value (LTV) and get 5 per cent cashback to spend as you choose. Some lenders offer much more than this.

Cashback is useful but often comes with redemption penalties. Most lenders will ask you to repay the money if you redeem in the early years so you may be better off just using your credit card for extra cash – especially if you choose one with a good introductory rate.

Firsts for first-timers

The first-time buyer market has seen a couple of innovations recently. The rent-a-room mortgage from the Marketplace at Bradford & Bingley allows you to take potential rental income into account when applying for a loan. For example, if you can get a lodger to pay £80 a week you can add £4,160 to your income, which means you can borrow about £13,520 more.

Another new scheme is Newcastle Building Society's Guarantor Mortgage. The lender takes into account money that can be guaranteed by a parent or relative. If you earn £20,000, Newcastle would typically offer you a mortgage of £80,000, but if the property you want to buy costs £100,000, it will let the £20,000 shortfall be guaranteed. Once you earn enough to take the mortgage on yourself, the guarantor will be relieved of their responsibility. You will still need a large deposit for the scheme – the maximum LTV is 85 per cent – but it could help you get your first home.

Shared ownership schemes

If house prices in your area make it difficult to afford your own home, find out if you can take advantage of a shared ownership scheme. Under this, you raise a mortgage to cover a proportion of the value of the property, and pay subsidised rent on the balance. You can increase your stake in the property after a year, and carry on doing so until you are the full owner.

Shared ownership schemes are run by housing associations and local councils. Most have long waiting lists and may give preference to those already renting council or housing association accommodation.

Each scheme has different criteria, but prospective buyers will generally need a regular income, and be required to complete a means test.

Shared ownership loans are available from around 20 lenders, including several High Street names. Most offer a range of loans, including fixed and discounted rates.

Right to Buy

If you have lived in a council property for two years or more you have a Right to Buy. You can either purchase outright or buy to rent on mortgage terms. That means you buy the property for less than the Right-to-Buy price with money from a lender, which will then charge repayments no more than your current rent. If you buy outright you will qualify for discounts, depending on length of tenancy and type of property. But as this book goes to press, Deputy Prime Minister, John Prescott, is reviewing the scheme.

With all these options, buying your first home may not be quite as hard as you first thought.

First home success with the Lambeth

In November, three important property market reports agreed that house price rises had probably peaked. For those wondering how on earth they can get on to the property ladder, after watching prices rise by 25 per cent in a year, such news may well have been a small crumb of comfort.

Even so, the situation is not helped by a shortage of affordable homes. High house prices have forced many key workers in education, the health service and the police to change jobs or live far away from where they work. In a move to ease the problem the government recently made funding available to Housing Associations wishing to build affordable properties.

Daunting though the property market must seem to so many, there are financial solutions for those looking to put a foot on the first rung of the home ownership ladder. One of these is Shared Ownership, the most widely offered Housing Association product.

In simple terms, Shared Ownership is a part-buy, part-rent scheme which enables you to buy a share as low as 25 per cent in a Housing Association home and pay a low rent on the rest. Then, if you wish, you can buy more shares until you own your home outright.

Shared Ownership is typically available on new houses, but increasingly many people find what they want through the resale market now that Housing Associations are refurbishing more and more older homes in established neighbourhoods.

A few Housing Associations operate a variation known as Do-It-Yourself Shared Ownership (DIYSO), a scheme that enables you to buy a home on the open market, up to a set value, anywhere in England. In other words, the property does not have to be one that an association has built or refurbished.

Another scheme is Homebuy. This is similar to DIYSO, except that you have to buy a fixed 75 per cent share in the property with the Housing Association making up the difference with a 25 per cent equity loan. Unlike Shared Ownership, there is no rent to pay and when you sell the property you receive three-quarters of the sale price, while the Housing Association gets its 25 per cent back in the form of the balance. At any time you can buy out its share at market value.

Some mortgage lenders specialise in schemes designed to help first-time buyers and key workers, usually offering loans of up to 95 per cent of the value of the purchaser's share. Lambeth, London's leading building society, took an early interest in Shared Ownership, and will consider applications not just from new borrowers in and around the capital, but nationwide. Wherever you live, it is easy to obtain in-principle decisions or make formal loan applications on-line via its website.

Unlike some lenders, Lambeth does not restrict first-time buyers to special products and you can choose any of the mortgage products it offers. It will provide first-time buyers with a decision in principle in an easy-to-understand, step-by-step process which makes budgeting easy.

Says Sean Wickes, Lambeth's General Manager, Sales & Marketing: "One of our prime goals has always been to help first-time buyers. This has led us, during the last year or so, to forge close links with several leading Housing Associations, particularly in London and the south east and, as a result, we have helped an even greater number of people take that important initial step towards owning their own home".

For further information call Lambeth Building Society on **020 7928 1331** or see its website at **www.lambeth.co.uk**

share your
dreams...

SHARED OWNERSHIP

If you want to buy a house but simply cannot afford to do so, help is at hand. Shared Ownership could get you that all-important first step on the housing ladder.

Andrew Theoff, a partner with The Parry Sharratt Partnership who are a firm of Solicitors specialising in acting for Housing Associations on Shared Ownership matters, explains what it is all about:

The concept of Shared Ownership has been around for over 20 years, but many people simply do not know of its existence or understand how it works. It is in fact very straight forward.

The house is bought by a Housing Association who then grant you a Shared Ownership Lease under which you buy a share in the property from them and pay rent on the remainder.

If therefore you buy a house for £150,000 but can only afford a mortgage of £75,000 you would buy a 50% Shared Ownership Lease. The price of your share is £75,000 and you would fund this by taking out a mortgage. The other 50% is rented from the Housing Association. What makes shared ownership more affordable than buying outright is that the rent which you pay is set at a low level and would cost less than borrowing the money from a mortgage company.

As your circumstances change and you are in a position to move up the housing ladder, you can increase your share via a procedure known as "staircasing". If you start off with a 50% Lease you could for example staircase up to 75% ownership and then up to full 100% ownership. These additional shares are paid for based on the market value at the time you staircase. Alternatively, if you want to move house, you can simply sell your shared ownership lease and then buy on the open market.

Shared ownership can take many different forms. The situation described above is known as DIYSO, which stands for Do It Yourself Shared Ownership. Many Housing Associations also develop new properties i.e. they build housing developments of their own. These new build properties are often sold on a shared ownership basis. Also, shared ownership properties often come up for sale, e.g. when a shared owner decides to move rather than staircase. Therefore, many Housing Associations have lists of properties that are up for sale and some high street Estate Agents have shared ownership properties on their books.

"Homebuy" is another scheme which is worth mentioning, although it is not strictly speaking shared ownership. With Homebuy you usually have to be able to fund at least 75% of the purchase price, but if you can it may well be a better option for you.

Under Homebuy, you do not part buy and part rent – the Housing Association simply lends you 25% of the purchase price. Their contribution is then secured on the property by way of a second Mortgage. You do not have to make any monthly payments to them, thus your outgoings would be less than if you bought 75% under shared ownership. The Housing Association's Mortgage is for 25% of the properties value at any given time. Therefore, when you come to sell the property (or if you want to pay off their loan) you would pay them 25% of what the property is worth at that time, which may be more or less than they lent you initially.

If an Association runs Shared Ownership or Homebuy there will be eligibility criteria to be met and most will have waiting lists. There is therefore no guarantee that this will be the solution for you. But if you have no other way of getting onto the housing ladder it is certainly well worth a try.

There are many Housing Associations up and down the country. They are non-profit making organisations, some of which are charities, and they are overseen by a government body known as the Housing Corporation. Details of a few Associations appear in this book, but otherwise try looking in the Yellow Pages for the ones nearest you.

THE PARRY·SHARRATT
PARTNERSHIP
SOLICITORS

Let a mortgage broker take the strain!

Arranging a mortgage can be a daunting task, so why not let a broker take the strain? Independent mortgage brokers such as Simply Homeloans have access to the market place as a whole, often including exclusive products not available on the high street. By using a mortgage broker to source your mortgage, you are taking away much of the stress associated with arranging your mortgage.

With over 200 lenders offering thousands of products in the UK, you may not be able to devote sufficient time to research them all. A good mortgage broker will be able to use their knowledge of the marketplace to suggest products that are best suited to your needs and situation. They will also be able to provide you with comparisons between products, ensuring you get the deal that is right for you and your budget. After all the lowest interest rate is not always the best deal!

Typically, mortgage brokers will charge a fee in the region of £195, although fees vary depending on the broker and type of mortgage you are applying for. By paying a fee, you can normally guarantee to receive impartial advice from an independent mortgage broker.

Mortgage brokers are able to obtain an agreement in principle, as well as completing and submitting mortgage applications electronically. With many lenders now embracing this new technology, the whole mortgage application process is faster, more efficient and improved over traditional methods.

As part of their service, brokers will make you aware of the importance of protecting your mortgage, by offering a range of associated products and services to ensure you, and your mortgage are protected whatever life throws at you. his is particularly important since the reduction in state support for mortgage holders.

Simply Homeloans

Relax!

At Simply Homeloans we have experts on hand to help you with a total home buying solution. From the day you decide to buy, to the day you are handed the keys; we're with you all the way.

Call our Advice Line free on
0800 138 3416

The mortgage specialists

www.simplyhomeloans.co.uk

6
Insurance

There are various types of insurance you will need to consider when buying a property and taking out a mortgage. This is a summary of the main points to take on board. You are likely to be offered various types of insurance by your lender, but they may not be particularly competitive. It is always worth checking if you can get cheaper cover elsewhere. Some lenders offer insurance cover as part of a mortgage, but this is rarely the best value. Check the terms of your employment before you buy cover. You may not need life cover, for example, if you are covered under your firm's pension scheme.

Buildings insurance

Buildings insurance covers you for damage to your property and any fixtures and fittings that you would not be able to take with you if you moved.

If you are buying a leasehold flat, you don't usually have to worry about taking out buildings insurance. The landlord generally arranges cover, with the cost included in the service charge. In most other cases, buildings insurance is your responsibility. Your lender will insist that you take out cover via them if you do not buy it elsewhere.

The cost of insurance will depend mainly on where you live. Premiums are likely to be higher than average if there is a history of subsidence in your area, or if you live on a flood plain. In the latter case, insurers may exclude damage caused by flooding altogether.

You need to insure for the cost of rebuilding, which is often higher than the market value of your property. The danger of under-insuring is that any claim you make could be scaled back in proportion.

Contents insurance

Contents insurance covers you for damage to the contents of your property. You don't have to buy it, but it makes sense to do so. The cost will depend on where you live, how much cover you want, and the type of cover you choose.

The following are some points to consider:

- Check what risks you are covered for. You may have to pay extra to get cover for accidental damage. Choose 'all risks' cover if you want to be insured against loss of, or damage to, valuable items you take out of your home.
- Be as accurate as possible about the value of your possessions, and insure for that amount. If you underinsure, you run the risk of a reduced pay-out if you make a claim.
- Think twice if the insurer insists on you taking security precautions, such as locking all windows or turning on an alarm. You could have a claim turned down if you don't stick to the agreed conditions.

Mortgage protection insurance

Mortgage protection insurance covers your mortgage payments for a set period if you are unable to pay due to accident, sickness or unemployment. You don't get much help from the State if you have problems paying your mortgage, so it is worth considering taking out insurance, but check carefully that any policy is suitable for your circumstances.

These are the main points to watch for:

- Self-employed people and short-term contract workers could find it hard to make a claim for unemployment.
- You will not be able to claim for any time off work due to an illness or disability that existed before you took out the policy.
- There is always a waiting period of 60 days before your policy will pay out after you make a claim.
- The policy will usually pay out for up to 12 months when you make a claim. Some insurers offer longer benefit periods.
- Expect to pay around £5 or £6 per £100 of payments you want to cover.

Life insurance

You need to take out life insurance if it is important that the mortgage will be paid off if you die, essentially if you have dependants.

- Choose *term assurance*, the cheapest type of life cover, which pays out if you die during the term of the policy, but gives nothing back if you don't.
- You want *level term cover* if you have an interest-only loan, or you can opt for decreasing term if you have a repayment mortgage.
- Couples get better value from *buying a policy each*, rather than one that covers them both.

Critical illness cover

Critical illness cover pays out a lump sum if you suffer any of the conditions named under the policy, such as cancer, a heart attack, or a stroke. The younger you are, the less you pay, so it is worth considering taking out a policy to cover your mortgage even if the possibility of claiming seems remote.

Permanent health insurance

Permanent health insurance (PHI) pays a monthly income if you cannot work because of ill health. Unlike mortgage protection insurance, it pays out until you go back to work, or to age 65 if you can't work at all. It is worth having, particularly for the self-employed. But it is expensive, and therefore unlikely to appear on the shopping list for most mortgage borrowers.

Landlord's insurance

If you are buying a property with the intention of letting it, your lender will require extra cover for home and contents, and this can work out around 50 per cent more than normal insurance premiums.

BUY TO LET – guaranteed return!

It is easy to assume that a buy-to-let investment will produce a guaranteed return ... prices are increasing, nothing that can go wrong!

But the performance of your investment depends largely on finding a responsible tenant who pays the rent. To start with all is well, but at the end of the second month, the rent does not arrive. Your tenant has lost his job or could just be repeating a well-rehearsed scam. You have no funds to pay your mortgage.

This all too common story, demonstrates that selecting the right tenant is vital and there are several suppliers who specialise in tenant referencing. So there is no excuse for not checking out your tenants before you sign-up the tenancy, and the cost of the check is immaterial when you think of the losses that you can suffer.

And there are ways of sharing the risk of your tenant not paying. Tenant referencing companies have developed rent guarantee products available where your tenant passes an assessment. It continues to pay the rent until vacant possession is gained and your property is ready to be let again.

As with all warranty products, each one has different levels of cover and exclusions, so read the small print and choose a reputable supplier who is a GISC (General Insurance Standards Council) member. Also be careful to select a product that covers all those responsible for paying the rent, as some policies may not offer this.

As an investment vehicle, buy-to-let is generally underpinned by capital growth over the longer term has been very reliable. With rent guarantee you can add some stability to your short-term returns as well.

The Liability of Being a Landlord

Its just like owning your own home, you just get insurance for the building, well the mortgage company insists on this, and perhaps you insure some of the contents. Oh no it is not!

Your tenants are great, they seem to be looking after your property like its their own, and the rent is paid exactly on time. Then there is accident – the rent stops being paid because your tenant cannot work – and they are taking an action against you as their landlord.

You read, probably for the first time, your owner-occupier policy and realise there is a vital omission; landlord liability cover is not included. Any landlord who carries this risk must be foolhardy in the extreme.

Landlord insurance remains a niche market, with specialist providers with policies that cover all the risks associated with letting. The premiums tend to be slightly higher to reflect the additional risks that are covered and most will provide between £5 million and £10 million of landlord liability.

Most good letting agents will be happy to recommend suitable policies, or go to a search engine on the web and search for "landlord insurance".

Your Tenants' Need Adequate Insurance Too

Many analysts suggest that "renters" are the wise ones nowadays as they have the mobility to allow them to chase the best jobs.

These tenants will probably have just the same possessions as owner-occupiers, but they also have the landlord's contents to consider. They need cover for items that they do not own, but for which they have responsibility through the tenancy agreement.

As a landlord do you really want to rely on the tenant's deposit to cover damage to your property? It is much more sensible to recommend to your tenant that they take adequate cover themselves.

Most insurers of tenant contents and personal possessions will allow the premium to be paid monthly. If you are going to recommend such a policy to your tenants, then look for those that do not charge ridiculous amounts for monthly payments.

Michael Arnold is a director of HomeLet, the UK's leading provider of tenant referencing and insurances for the letting industry. HomeLet's products are available through some 5,000 letting agents nationwide.

7
Making the move

Buying a property and moving in is definitely up there on the list of life's most stressful events. So anything you can do to make the process run smoothly is good news. Here are the main steps to follow.

Obtain a mortgage offer in principle

Ideally, this should be done before you start looking for a home. That's because it gives you an idea of how much you can afford. It also establishes you as a more serious home purchaser with estate agents you contact. If you haven't obtained an offer-in-principle yet, do it as soon as possible.

Find a solicitor

The moment you make an offer and it is accepted, you need to tell the estate agent who your solicitor is, so that he or she can pass the details to the vendor's own lawyers. Find a lawyer before you make the offer, or straight after. Always get a quote from several before choosing one. Make sure you are comparing like with like: does the quote include search fees, VAT, phone calls, letters and postage, or bank transfer fees?

Find a house and make a bid

Offer what you think the property is worth. Make the offer subject to a survey of the property. If the price is marginally above a stamp duty cut-off point (see table below), offer slightly below this amount to save money. Where necessary, exclude the cost of carpets, curtains and other fixtures from the purchase price to do this.

Stamp duty	£ (%)
Up to £60,000	nil
£60,001 to £250,000	1%
£250,001 to £500,000	3%
£500,001 and above	4%

Contact lender and arrange survey

Once you have had an offer accepted, you need to finalise details with your lender and organise a survey. There are three main types of survey:

- The lender will demand a Mortgage Valuation. You will normally pay for this, but it is commissioned by the lender. It's a brief report on the property you plan to buy, basically telling the lender whether or not it is worth the money you have offered.
- It's highly advisable to commission your own survey, known as a Homebuyer's Report. This is likely to cost two or three hundred pounds, but it's much more detailed than the valuation and it's a direct contract between you and the surveyor. This should pick up any problems – like a bad roof or damp – that might lead you to lower the offer you've made on the property. You can ask the lender's surveyor to make a Homebuyer's Report at the same time he or she does the valuation. Or you can commission an independent surveyor.
- For complete peace of mind a full Structural Survey may be necessary. This is the most expensive kind of survey, but it includes full details of all visible parts of the house, and highlights defects.

All surveyors only look at visible things – they don't lift carpets, for example – so you may well move into your new home and find things that have not been picked up.

Some surveyors in 'hot spots' such as London will value property at less than its market price. This is a problem for you if you are borrowing a high percentage of the cost of the property, because the lender will go on the surveyor's valuation – not what you have paid in the real market. You may end up losing the property, or being asked to pay a high lending fee (also known as a mortgage indemnity guarantee).

Think about what you need from a surveyor

Before you fork out, it is worth taking the time to think about what it is you want the survey to tell you.

Your requirements will be different if you are simply moving house than if you are looking to renovate or restore a property.

If you do have a specific requirement from your surveyor, for example, if you are buying an older home or a listed building, it is worthwhile finding a surveyor who has some degree of experience or speciality in that field.

What can a surveyor do?

If you have any plans for renovating the property, your surveyor is the best source of information for the viability of the work you plan. He or she can provide you with information and advice about:

- planning permission – What are the restrictions? Are there any fees?
- demolition and erection of structural walls and other major changes;
- listed building regulations – guidelines and limitations;
- conservation area regulations and levels of restriction;
- safety issues.

Finding a surveyor

If you have chosen to undertake a survey of a property independently of your mortgage provider, it is worth spending the time making sure the surveyor will provide what you need from a survey.

The better way to sell and buy your home!

by Christopher Legrand, FRICS

Surveyors and Valuers Accreditation Ltd

On 13th November 2002 Her Majesty the Queen referred to a Housing Bill in her speech at the State Opening of Parliament. This Bill will contain fundamental reforms to the home buying and selling process in England and Wales.

Research shows that up to 30% of house sales and purchases fall through between the acceptance of an offer from a buyer and exchange of binding contracts, at an estimated loss of £350 million a year to those who are collectively affected by these stressful and wasteful events. The majority of people move home only a few times in their lives and are inclined to put their strained experiences down to 'bad luck', however the figures given above show that 'bad luck' occurs all too often and reform is long overdue.

The changes are expected to come into operation in late 2005 or the first part of 2006, allowing the property industry to gear up and adapt to the changes, which have a lot to do with improvements in 'information and communication technology'.

In the meantime, however, forward thinking estate agents, surveyors, conveyancers and other linked businesses have launched voluntary initiatives to help sellers and buyers, and these are going very well with much consumer acceptance and support.

So what are the reforms?

The raft of reforms includes electronic conveyancing, faster searches, simpler forms, on line information and faster mortgage offers. Buyers will be able to get mortgage certificates from lenders telling them what they can borrow before they go house hunting.

However the most important change to affect home sellers and buyers is the requirement, by law, for the seller or their agent, to put together a pack of information about the home they are selling, **before they commence to market it to potential buyers**. Whilst this may sound complicated, the only differences to what happens today are that first, the information currently requested by a buyer or their conveyancer is, under the planned legislation, put together before the property is marketed, rather than a few days before contracts are due for exchange. Second, there is one addition to the information currently provided.

The property will be marketed with a 'Home Condition Report', a report prepared by a Licensed Home Inspector, upon which the buyer is entitled to rely, and for which insurance backing is available. The availability of this report will enabling buyers and sellers to reach agreement in full knowledge of the physical facts about the property.

Home buyers need to know that report is reliable. It is prepared to satisfy the requirements of the legislation, not the requirements of the seller. It is specifically designed with consumers, (that is everyone involved in the transaction) in mind, and is produced by a fully tested and licensed Home Inspector who works to National Occupational Standards. The conduct and competence of Home Inspectors will be constantly monitored.

The basis of the report is made clear to all parties and sellers, buyers and lenders will be able to rely on it. Its existence does not prevent buyers from commissioning their own independent enquiries, if they so wish.

The advantages of the changes are that sellers and buyers are much better informed about what is often the largest transaction in their lives, and all the information required to complete the transaction is available for conveyancers to work on as soon agreement is reached between the parties.

Overall, the proposals are designed to take much of the stress and frustration out of home buying and selling as well as reducing the number of transactions that fail and the huge amount of wasted costs.

Surveys are expensive and can be very important when deciding whether to go ahead with a sale so don't be afraid to ask questions. Many surveyors have areas of speciality, which may suit your needs better. For example, they may specialise in listed buildings or auction properties.

Chartered Surveyors

Members and Affiliates of the Royal Institution of Chartered Surveyors (RICS) can be identified by the letters MRICS and FRICS (Fellow of the Royal Institution of Chartered Surveyors) after their name. They are the only people allowed to call themselves Chartered Surveyors or Chartered Building Surveyors.

Sellers' packs

Government proposals for Sellers' Packs (SPs) could change the way we buy and sell property in England and Wales. The aim is to shift responsibility for gathering information and getting a survey done from the buyer to the seller, and thereby speed up the buying process. But, of course, this will cost, and the current price quoted is between £700 and £1,200 to sell the average home. Most estate agents are against the idea, describing it as bureaucratic and unenforceable. They say the expense of a Sellers' Pack will put people off moving. The Government has already been forced to back down on one key proposal – ministers have cancelled plans to make it a criminal offence to advertise a house for sale without a current SP. The target introduction date has not yet been finalised, but is likely to be sometime during 2006.

Exchange contracts/complete

The standard gap between exchanging contracts and completion is 30 days, but it can be longer or shorter. You can ask your solicitor to put a clause into the contract stipulating a time limit. Points to check include the following:

- Make sure that all the legal paperwork is properly sorted. Don't be afraid to ask about any point you don't understand. If you have paid a deposit (usually between 5 and 10 per cent) you will lose it if you pull out after exchange.
- Check and check again that the funds are ready to be paid by your lender into the vendor's account, via your solicitor. Failure to do so means you won't be able to move in.

You are now ready to move into your house. You should already have hired a removal firm. Be sure to compare prices and make sure your chosen firm is insured if anything is lost or broken.

Contact electricity, gas, water and phone companies to let them know you are moving to a new address – give meter readings for both the old and the new address. Now is the time to decide who you want to supply your energy, water and phone needs at your new address.

Completion will take place when all legal questions have been agreed and the cash has been passed on to the seller from your lender, via your own and his/her solicitor.

8
Buy-to-let

Buying property to let is becoming increasingly popular. There's now a whole army of amateur landlords out there depending on their investment in bricks and mortar to finance their retirement.

Low mortgage rates and the availability of buy-to-let mortgages have made it an option for many more people. The main attraction is the potential for a better return than on other investments like stocks and shares.

What you might get back

You can expect rental income to provide a return on your investment of 7 or 8 per cent on average, before costs.

You may also make a capital gain on your property. Property prices generally rise faster than inflation, and have averaged a gain of 8.9 per cent a year over the last 25 years. However, this also includes a period in the late-1980s/early-1990s when prices fell.

Using a mortgage to fund your purchase gives you a 'geared' investment that can magnify returns enormously. For example, say you put down a deposit of £10,000 on a £100,000 property, the rent covers all outgoings, and after five years you sell the property for £150,000. The gains you have made before tax are £50,000. This equals a return of 500 per cent on your original investment.

There is a risk, though. Gearing magnifies losses as well. If property prices fall, you could go into negative equity, owing more on your mortgage than the property is worth.

Thinking of letting your property?

If so, for peace of mind use an agent who is a member of The National Approved Letting Scheme.

The National Approved Letting Scheme (NALS) is a voluntary accreditation scheme for lettings and management agents. It was established in 1999 with the objective of giving owners the confidence to let their property by appointing qualified agents who in joining the Scheme, have agreed to abide by a set of minimum service standards for letting and management.

The NALS Scheme was set up to provide much needed benchmark service standards that would enable landlords and tenants to avoid the pitfalls of dealing with rogue letting agents.

The Scheme backed by the Government and the professional bodies in the lettings sector ARLA (Association of Residential Letting Agents), NAEA (National Association of Estate Agents) and RICS (Royal Institution of Chartered Surveyors) is open to any agent in the lettings sector who meets the strict criteria for accreditation.

It is a prerequisite of membership that firms should have in place a customer complaints procedure underpinned by an arbitration scheme, Professional Indemnity insurance and Client Money Protection insurance which ensures that clients' money is protected.

For further information on NALS and to obtain details of an agent in your area contact:
The National Approved Letting Scheme
Warwick Corner
42 Warwick Road
Kenilworth CV8 1HE
T: 01926 866633 F: 01926 866644
E-mail: info@nalscheme.co.uk
Website: www.nalscheme.co.uk

Do your sums

The possibility of falling property prices is only one of the factors you need to consider. There are plenty of others that will have an impact on any total return to be made on property. Here are some of them:

- *Agency fees*: using a letting agent to manage your property will cost between 10 and 15 per cent of rental income.
- *Income tax*: rent counts as income, which you should declare on a self-assessment tax form each year. You can offset various expenses against tax, including mortgage interest, agent's fees, the cost of repairs, and expenses associated with a leasehold flat (typically ground rent, service charges and buildings insurance).
- *Capital gains tax (CGT)*: if the property is not your main place of residence you may be liable to CGT on any profit you make when it is sold. There are some exemptions that could apply to you. Talk to a tax specialist.
- *Insurance*: lenders will almost certainly require extra cover if you propose to let the property. It is generally at least 50 per cent dearer than normal home and contents insurance.
- *Maintenance*: most property letting agents advise that at least 10 per cent of monthly income ought to be kept back for property repairs and maintenance.
- *Void periods*: this is the time between tenancies when you will not be able to collect any rent. Agents suggest you allow for a void period of two months in each year.
- *A rise in interest rates*: will you be able to meet the extra costs if this happens – or raise your tenants' rent to cover your costs?
- *Diversification*: consider if you want such a sizeable chunk of your total wealth portfolio to be in property.

You must take a long-term view if you decide to buy a property to rent out. A minimum of five years is a good rule of thumb – it is not a way of getting rich quick. The above questions don't negate the value of property as an investment, so don't let the issues put you off, but do think carefully before making such an important decision.

Common mistakes

There are three mistakes amateur landlords are most likely to make:

First mistake

The first mistake most of them make is looking and buying a property they would like to live in themselves. But the rental market is different from the owner-occupied market and tenants don't want the same things as owners. Buying a property to rent out as an investment is a business decision. Buying a home to live in is an emotional decision. The two are not the same.

For example, tenants don't look for 'character', 'original fixtures', 'history' or 'community feeling'. They do care about good public transport links, size of bedrooms (important when it comes to splitting the rent) and being able to move straight in to a low maintenance place.

Second mistake

Most amateur landlords spend too much money fitting out their property. Especially if the house or flat is to be rented out to two or more tenants, most items will have to be replaced after each tenancy ends and the place redecorated. This is not because the tenants will be irresponsible or wreckers, but simply because of wear and tear. And you are much more likely to rent it quickly if would-be tenants are impressed by a freshly-decorated, spick and span place.

Dos and don'ts include:

● Don't spend money on an expensive dinner service – just go to a High Street shop and buy plain white china.

- Don't spend time agonising over paint colours – just decorate with white paint throughout.
- Don't buy top-of-the-range beds and mattresses expecting them to last – buy a cheap mattress at the beginning of each tenancy.
- Do spend money on a decent shower. If the bathroom needs replacing do it with a white suite.
- Don't bother with carpet. Tiles or easily-replaceable and cleaned lino is better.
- Do update the kitchen if it needs it – again keep it simple.
- Do comply with all safety regulations and make sure everything works – the heating, the electrics, the oven – and do get all the relevant safety checks done by a CORGI registered gas engineer. All the furniture also has to comply with the Furnishings Fire and Safety Regulations 1988. Make sure everything you buy – mattresses, sofas, curtains and upholstery – have passed the flammability tests and are labelled as such. The fine for not doing so is £5,000. Don't forget smoke detectors and fire extinguishers either.

Third mistake

Many new landlords think they can find the tenants themselves. They either want to save the money a letting agency would charge or they have a friend of a friend move in. But using an approved letting agent is the best way of ensuring that any prospective tenant is financially sound, with all references properly checked. This sets you up for a hassle-free tenancy.

There are two organisations – the Association of Residential Lettings Agents (ARLA) and the National Approved Lettings Scheme (NALS) – that offer protection to landlords and tenants from cowboy rental companies. The average fee is 10 per cent to find and check out a tenant, get the deposit and draw up the tenancy agreement. That's a small price to pay for peace of mind.

Remember, renting out a property is a formal business arrangement. Even the friend of a friend should sign a standard rental agreement. An

Assured Shorthold Tenancy contract means that you can give the tenant notice to quit after six months if something goes wrong. You can buy them from good stationers.

At the end of the tenancy be fair and realistic about returning the renter's deposit. The deposit is usually between six and eight weeks' rent so it's a sizeable sum. You cannot hold back £50 because the number of spoons is down. You can withhold the cost of having the place cleaned if it's left dirty on departure. You cannot charge the tenant for normal wear and tear – be professional.

Watch out for new rules and regulations

Regulations going through parliament may make it more expensive for small landlords to let their properties. Some industry experts say the regulations – contained in a private member's bill with Government support – could lead to the closure of some of Britain's estimated 1.5 million 'houses in multiple occupation', or HMOs. These are defined as properties occupied 'by persons who do not form a single household'. There are eight types but they fit into two broad categories:

- houses converted into bed-sits, flats or private rooms with communal areas but just one front door and one landlord;
- unconverted houses with individuals having their own rooms, but almost all other spaces shared by three or more people, such as students or young professionals.

The Department of Transport, Local Government and the Regions (DTLR) – which oversees regulation for the private rented sector – says it is likely to become law after its passage through parliament this year, 2003.

It requires landlords or managing agents to fit extensive health and safety measures, which may include additional bathrooms, fire escapes and energy conservation features. It also introduces a national licensing system for HMOs, making safety checks and a licence mandatory before a landlord can rent to sharers.

Property professionals say the measures will be useful for forcing up the standards of unscrupulous landlords who exploit vulnerable tenants, but some fear they may deter small investors who buy-to-let as an alternative to a pension, as well as those who take lodgers. More licence fees, more regulations and more work required will eat into profit margins unless rents are raised.

Costs will obviously vary according to the size and condition of each house. A conventional house (even in good condition) may require more than £8,000 of work to reach an adequate standard, plus extra annual surveys and repair bills thereafter.

Similar constraints exist in Scotland, where the Edinburgh parliament has passed legislation introducing strict controls over properties with three or more sharers.

Taxes

The downside of investing in property is that all forms of income, including that from bricks and mortar, are liable for income tax. And if the rental property is sold, any profit may also be subject to capital gains tax. But the upside is that landlords can deduct a number of expenses from the rent that tenants pay, so only the profit is taxed.

The tax return deadline

If you receive any income at all from property, you must remember to fill out the relevant land and property pages on your tax return and submit it all to the Inland Revenue by 31 January. This is the date when any tax you owe must also be paid; otherwise you'll face a fine and possible surcharges.

Everyone who had an income from property in the year running from 6 April 2001 to 5 April 2002 should have received a tax return. This comprises the standard form plus additional property pages. If you haven't received all this, get in touch with the Revenue immediately, as not receiving a tax return is not a legitimate excuse for failing to submit it on time.

Getting started

Once you have the forms you need, filling them out should be straight-forward as long as you have all your accounts, bank statements and receipts to hand. If your gross income from property was less than £15,000, it should be even easier as all you have to supply is a figure for your total profit (income less expenses).

All rental activities are aggregated and treated as if they constitute a single business, so if you have several properties, the income and costs from all of them should be added together. The advantage of this arrangement is that if you made a big profit on one address, it should go some way to balancing out the losses made on another.

All rent, whether from furnished or unfurnished property, is regarded as income, as are separate charges to tenants for the hiring of furniture, and service charges to meet the landlord's responsibility for maintaining common parts of a building.

Deductible expenses

It is possible to reduce your taxable profit via a number of deductible expenses. The rent is included in this but the cost of buying the property isn't. Most landlords opt for an interest-only mortgage because all your monthly payments can be offset against tax.

With a repayment mortgage, where part of the capital is paid back along with interest on the loan each month, it is still possible to deduct expenses but only from the interest part – and the sums become more complicated. Several expenses are normally deductible when calculating the profits of your rental business. Council tax, insurance premiums – both buildings and contents insurance and cover for the non-payment of rent – and advertising costs can all be claimed.

Travelling expenses incurred by the landlord when checking the property, to carry out repairs or collect the rent, are also allowable deductions. If you travel by car, it is likely that you are also using it at other times, in which case you have to work out the proportion of the running costs attributable to business use.

Repairs or improvements?

The cost of repairs can be claimed back against the rent, but landlords need to be careful because capital expenditure, in the form of most improvements, isn't tax deductible. For example, if you touch up the property with a lick of paint when you first buy it, you can claim the cost of this back against the rent. But if you buy a dilapidated property that requires thousands of pounds' worth of work before you can let it, the cost of those improvements is regarded as a capital expense and can't be claimed against the rent.

In general, any work that isn't strictly necessary but increases the value of the property, such as a new fitted kitchen or conservatory, is considered to be capital expenditure and can't be claimed back.

Furnished property

If your property is furnished, there are other allowable expenses. You can't claim for the cost of actually buying the beds, sofa or washing machine, but you can claim the subsequent cost of replacing damaged or worn-out furniture and furnishings.

Landlords can choose to deduct 10 per cent of the rent, net of council tax, from income as a wear-and-tear allowance. Or you can deduct the full cost of renewing individual items such as chairs and rugs, as and when the expenditure is incurred. Whichever method you choose, it must be used consistently and you are not allowed to chop and change from year to year.

Making life easier

One way to minimise the hassle of keeping your own accounts is to employ a letting agent. This can be time and cost effective because as they are managing the property for you, they will also be able to tell you how much income you have received and what expenses have been incurred.

Many people are put off employing a letting agent by the costs involved, which can be up to 15 per cent of the rent for a full management service. However, these fees are tax deductible, so you can both get your money back and reduce the accounting hassle.

Going it alone shouldn't be a problem as long as you protect yourself by maintaining accurate records and keeping all receipts, bank statements and invoices for at least six years – the Revenue can make random enquiries of any taxpayer.

What happens when you sell?

Your 'principal private residence' is exempt from capital gains tax (CGT), but higher-rate taxpayers are potentially liable for CGT at 40 per cent on the profits from the sale of a holiday cottage or a buy-to-let property. Basic-rate taxpayers pay CGT at 20 per cent.

However, there is an easy way to cut – or even eliminate – your tax bill. If you have two properties, you can choose which is your main residence for tax purposes. But you must make your choice within two years of buying the second home – and you must at some point have lived in the property.

As long as you meet the deadline, you can change your mind later and elect the other property – with no time limit. The rule means that you may be able to minimise CGT on the sale of a second home.

Suppose you bought a buy-to-let six years ago for £100,000 and are now selling it for £200,000. Taper relief reduces the chargeable gain the longer you have held the asset, and after six years you would pay CGT on 80 per cent of the profit. A higher-rate taxpayer would therefore pay

40 per cent tax on £80,000 (£32,000). However, if you had met the two-year deadline, you could now nominate the cottage as your principal private residence for a week, then re-elect the first property.

If the property has been nominated as your main residence, even for such a short time, the last three years are always exempt from CGT. In other words, half the profits will be tax-free. If you bought your second property more recently, you may be able to avoid CGT altogether.

For more information contact: the Association of Residential Letting Agents (ARLA), www.arla.co.uk or 0845 345 5752; www.inlandrevenue.gov.uk or try its self-assessment helpline on 0845 900 0444, open evenings and weekends.

To Buy to Let – that is the question

With the recent turbulence in the stock markets and the consistent rise in property values, it is hardly surprising that investors have turned to property as their preferred investment option.

The Buy to Let market has, as a result, been growing at a substantial rate. Figures produced by the Council of Mortgage Lenders reported that, during the first half of 2002, there were more than 58,000 buy to let loans worth £5.5 billion taken out. This represents an increase of 38% on the preceding 6 months.

Despite the rumourmongers that the buy to let bubble is about to burst, we still haven't heard any bang! Many experts believe that buying a property to rent out continues to be a good investment prospect over the long term and, according to a recent report by ARLA (the Association of Residential Letting Agents), investors can expect to achieve rental returns of between 4% and 7%, depending on the area in which the property is located.

A buy to let property will not normally be an investor's main residence so careful consideration needs to be given as to how the purchase will be financed.

Arranging a mortgage on a buy to let property can be quite simple as there is very little difference in process to arranging a mortgage on a home that you will live in. As the buy to let market has grown, so has the number of mortgage products that are available, so there is a relatively good range, at attractive rates to choose from. There are many lenders that offer these types of products.

Lenders will normally allow borrowing up to 85% of the property's value, so a minimum 15% deposit needs to be found. Rather than basing your ability to pay on personal income, lenders will normally assess the loan on the rental income that the property can achieve. Generally speaking, therefore, the gross rent aimed for should be between 115% and 150% of the monthly mortgage payment. To get an idea of what the rental might be on a chosen property, a rental quotation can be obtained from an ARLA-registered agent, details of which can be found on their web site www.arla.co.uk

GMAC Residential Funding is an appointed ARLA lender and offers several buy to let products: these range from fixed rates to trackers, which follow a market-recognised rate plus a fixed margin. We are also able to offer mortgage products to people who may have had previous credit difficulties. All of our mortgage products have an additional benefit, which allows the investor to build a portfolio of investment properties, up to a total value of £2 million.

As with any investment though, buying a property to let should be viewed as a medium to long-term proposition and potential investors should always take a realistic view of the risks – such as a potential decrease in the property value – as well as the rewards. It is always a good idea to take expert advice on what will be involved, such as costs, tax, legal issues and so on, before entering into any investment transaction.

You find the right property...

...we've got the right mortgage

A mortgage that asks for:

- rental income of the property, not what you earn

- minimal paperwork for a faster turnaround

- a minimum deposit of 15%

And allows you to take on additional properties up to a total of £2 million.

To find out more contact your independent financial adviser or mortgage broker. Alternatively, call 0800 731 0137.

GMAC Residential Funding

A General Motors company

Mortgages for everyone

A member of

ARLA

9
Self-build

Building your own home

Self-build is a tiny part of the housing market in the UK. Last year, the Nationwide, Britain's biggest building society, financed just 600 projects throughout the country. But the idea of building your own home is becoming increasingly popular as we strive to find the house of our dreams. Between 20,000 and 25,000 people build their own homes every year, and of those 90 per cent have never built anything before.

How to get a self-build mortgage

Most of us delude ourselves into believing we own our house. Of course, that's not true. The lender owns it usually for the first 25 years we live there. A bank or a building society pays upfront and then sells the place back to you in stages, so that you can move in decades before you'd otherwise have been able to afford to.

But if, as is the case with a self-build, there's no house for the mortgage lender to buy upfront, you can forgive them for wondering where their money's going. You're going to have to do a lot more talking than usual to convince them you're a good risk.

Lenders, perhaps justifiably, believe more can go wrong with a self-build than a traditional house purchase. This is why self-build mortgages come with a much tighter web of checks and controls. Many lenders won't give you a penny until your building is up to first-floor level.

Lenders generally won't give you a cheque for the cost of buying some land and building a house, and then leave you to get on with it. Often they will expect you to have found and bought the land already.

Some lenders refuse to handover any cash for the site. If they are willing to do so, it's unlikely to be more than 75 per cent, but at least that way you know they're interested in doing business with self-builders.

Your ultimate aim is to get the best deal on offer so you have to look for a variety of features, not least the amount they're willing to lend you in the first place. Each lender has a percentage of your property's projected value it is willing to stump up – this is known as the loan to value ratio (LTV), and will typically be around 75 to 95 per cent.

As with all other mortgages, the lender will only give you a loan it's confident you'll be able to repay, so look at three times your own annual income, plus one times your partner's, if applicable, and that's your maximum loan.

A good way of finding out about all the deals on offer is to get hold of a monthly magazine called *Moneyfacts*. It's available by subscription from your local newsagents. *Moneyfacts* will tell you exactly what rates are on offer from the various lenders, allowing you to weigh up the alternatives.

As a self-builder you need to ask a lot more questions because mortgage companies like to tailor each deal to the individual project. This is their way of making sure their investment is sound. The most obvious way they can do this is by strong control of the purse strings. Self-build mortgages pay out in stages. Each lender does this a different way, but typical stages include the completion of foundations, weatherproofing, damp course, first floor and so on. These are usually called 'progress' or 'instalment' mortgages.

The theory is that this way, you're given just enough money to stay ahead of the game, while the lender's commitment only goes up as the value of your site increases. The majority of failures among self-build mortgages happen at this stage – and it's not normally the self-builder's fault. Contractors going bust is the main problem.

Once the house is complete, you can move over to a traditional repayment plan, taking up the mortgage to suit your needs.

One of the most self-build-friendly lenders is the Bradford & Bingley, which recognises the unique problems associated with building your own home. 'Cash flow has dogged self-builders for years,' says the company's specialist in the field. 'It's been a question of beg, borrow and steal money to see you through until you can get the funds released.'

In response, it set up what it calls an Accelerator Mortgage, in conjunction with the Self-Build Advisory Service (SBAS). This enables self-builders to borrow up to 95 per cent of the build costs. Normally, if, for example, you're buying a kit home, you have to finance the purchase of the kit before it's been erected. With this mortgage, once the kit has been delivered on site, they'll advance 95 per cent of the cost of purchasing it. This gets over a lot of cash-flow problems.

Other costs

Apart from the price of the plot and your build costs, other expenses to take into consideration are architect's fees, service connections, special groundworks, garden landscaping, insurance and administration costs.

The fee for drawing up your house plans can vary from a few hundred pounds, if done by a draftsman, to several thousand if you decide to use an architect.

Expect to pay at least £1000 for connection fees to electricity, water, sewerage and gas, and considerably more if your plot is off the beaten track.

Steep sites and soft ground can create problems requiring specialist foundations so this should be taken into account as well.

Landscaping for your garden is usually best done at the outset so should also be included in the equation.

Another hefty expense is the cost of insurance, which will probably set you back around £1,500.

Finally, remember that while all the building is going on you will need to live somewhere – rented accommodation or an on-site caravan. These costs also should be taken into account and there are several excellent software packages to help you calculate your costs and projected cash-flow.

Finding a plot

Finding a plot for your new house can be a frustrating and time-consuming process. Also, it is very much a case of chicken and egg. Which comes first – finding a plot and then choosing a house design or choosing the house design and finding a plot that suits it?

Both methods have their 'pros' and 'cons'. What use is a plot in an excellent location if it isn't wide enough for your new home? Or you could plan your dream mansion and never find a plot that will do it justice.

As always the answer is to compromise. Look for plots and consider the type of house that can be built on it. In many cases a plot may be found between two other houses, in which case planning permission may only be granted if your home fits in with local architecture. What benefit is there in having a plan for a contemporary glass and steel structure when it will sit between two thatched cottages?

The size of the plot required can be predicted by knowing how big the house will be and whether you need a large garden or a garage.

So, what should you consider as the most important aspect of your plot? The answer to this will also influence how you find your plot – location. If you want to live locally, you have an advantage in that you will probably know who the local estate agents are, receive the local paper and may even see plots for sale as you drive around. If your chosen area is on the other side of the country, you will need to investigate the available plot-finding resources very carefully.

Where to find a plot

The obvious first place to look for plots is the estate agents. The large chains may be helpful if your plot searching campaign is centred elsewhere in the country, as they can put you in touch with their other offices.

Some estate agents have extensive lists of plots and go to a great deal of trouble to provide information, pictures and maps of where they are.

Others either have no plots at all or regard them as a secondary issue to selling houses. The larger chains will often have a 'land and new homes division', while the smaller agents may not sell a plot from one year to the next.

Don't be content being put on an agent's mailing list. Keep in regular contact with them, especially just prior to the local newspaper going on sale – any new plots they are to advertise in the paper can be checked out before the rest of the readership even knows about it.

Surveyors, architects, architectural technicians and planning consultants can also provide leads on land for sale. Such professions revolve around building sites and future developments. Chances are one of them might know of something in the pipeline.

It's the same for friends, neighbours and colleagues. If you tell enough people that you are looking for a plot in a particular area, someone somewhere will know about one, or suggest a potential site. A conversation in the pub over a pint could end months of searching. It's worth a try.

The local newspapers advertise plots of land but you have to be quick to get the good ones. You could always run a 'building plot wanted' advertisement in the paper. State what you want, for example, a plot suitable for a bungalow, with planning permission, rural location, and where you want it. Not only will those people with plots for sale be interested, but those with land not yet for sale may contact you out of the blue.

Check also the official notices in the classified section. Many councils put notices of planning applications in the local papers in addition to posting notices of the application to the neighbours of the site. As a result, you may be able to scoop a plot before it goes on the market.

Auctions

Newspapers will also advertise forthcoming auctions in your area. Often sourced from bankruptcies and mortgage foreclosures, this is a chance to find plots that would not ordinarily come on to the market and may be cheaper than market value.

To find out about what is coming up for sale in the next few weeks, Faxwise (020 7720 5000) provides a subscription service called 'auction watch', which will inform you of any lots. *SelfBuild & Design* contains a comprehensive list of plot details in the back of each issue. It is an invaluable guide to land prices and availability in all areas of the country, as well as a listing of those estate agents who deal with building land.

If your house is to be built by a package company, it is in their interests for you to find a plot. Some companies have land lists. Speak to them to see if they can offer assistance in finding a plot, but don't let their answer cloud your judgement. Just because they know of plots for sale doesn't mean they can build the right house for you.

Exhibitors at the various self-build shows and exhibitions may also have local knowledge of plots. The more local the show, the greater the chance of coming across a contact.

Builders and developers are self-builders on a major scale. They buy in bulk, purchasing development sites of several acres to build a set number of homes. In many cases they will have a few spaces on the site that are not utilised in their plans. These present ideal opportunities for the canny self-builder, as the developer will receive cash for a piece of land they were going to leave bare, while you get a plot, often with planning permission and services on site.

Councils also own areas of land that they sell off occasionally for extra cash. In some cases, tenancy of the land has ended and the council will prefer to sell. In other cases, council policy may change, prompting the sale. The council may also own buildings that can be converted or renovated. Call the estates department to find out if any property is coming up for sale in the near future.

Utility companies and large businesses may also have land for sale. Railtrack, British Gas, the electricity and water companies, even breweries often have land surplus to requirements.

Finally, if your own efforts fail, try the professionals. There are several plotfinding companies that will produce a list of plots to meet your criteria – for a fee. At the end of the day, there is no secret to finding your ideal plot. Some self-builders find land amazingly easily and can start their project straight away. Others may look for several years. Whatever the circumstances, perseverance is vital.

Planning permission

Plots with planning permission are more expensive as they have already been permitted to become potential homes. A plot without planning permission is just a bare piece of land. Don't be fooled into buying it on the off-chance you can build on it. If it's not sold with outline planning permission, the vendor is missing out on extra cash so there must be a reason for it.

What is it?

There are two types of planning permission – outline (OPP) and detailed (DPP). Outline, as its name implies, means that the planning department has agreed the basics of a development proposal. The usual routine is that once OPP has been granted, you apply for DPP or reserved matters. This is only given when the planning department has agreed exactly what can be built on your plot using your detailed house plans as their guide. Even building materials and height can influence a decision at this point.

So if you are trying to get DPP why bother going through the process of applying for OPP? In many cases plots will already have OPP, which means that while the plot can be built on, the style of house remains open. Alternatively, applying for OPP will save you the cost of having expensive house plans drawn up before you are even sure you are allowed to build at all.

With OPP you can put forward as many detailed applications as you like. An interesting point is that you don't have to own the land to make an application, so you can find out if you can build on a plot before making an offer on it.

Once you have OPP, you have three years in which to make reserved matters before having to re-apply. Reserved matters is the term for a follow-on application to outline planning. Detailed planning, however, can slightly alter what was originally proposed as the planning committee will reassess the application. Having gained DPP you have five years in which to begin work on a development.

Even with OPP, detailed planning doesn't always come easy. Permission usually depends on a number of conditions, such as the colour of brick, the type of roofing material, even the size and location of windows. These conditions usually come about due to the council's concern that new housing will look out of place or interfere with established homes.

How do you get it?

Firstly, you need to apply for it. In theory, this is just a case of filling in some forms, but the reality is that this matter deserves plenty of time and effort to get it right first time. Having decided what you want, a house of a particular size or an extension for example, you can do plenty of research prior doing the actual paperwork.

The Local Plan at your council's planning office will show you what areas are deigned as favourable for development. Make sure your proposals fall into line with it, and while there is a chance that the plan will change, these things tend to take a very long time.

Professionals such as building surveyors, architects or architectural technicians will be helpful at this early stage to guide you through the intricacies of the planning process and later prepare technical drawings.

You should also contact the local planning officer to discuss the proposal prior to application. This will give you an insight into how favourably the planning department will look on your application. If you are using an architect or surveyor, bring them along to the meeting. You should receive some feedback with suggestions as to what might need rethinking – blocking light into a neighbour's living room, for example.

Detailed planning permission has a standard fee for each dwelling, whereas outline planning is charged depending upon the size of the proposed development site.

With the application you should state whether you own all, part or none of the site and whether it has agricultural tenancy. If you are not the sole owner, then the actual owner must be notified of your intention.

A location map, usually OS 1:2,500 or 1:1,250, should accompany the application. For DPP, a site plan should also be included, alongside floor plans and all elevations showing the front, back and side views. If your proposed house is to be supplied by a kit-home manufacturer, they will usually supply the floor plans and elevations.

A number of copies of the application plans and drawings will need to be sent to the planning office. Once processed, the council will inform neighbours of your proposal and tell them where they can see the plans and how long they have to give their opinions – usually 21 days from receiving the letter.

The outcome of a planning application can go four ways: refusal, delegated, deferred or permission granted. *Refusal* is the worst that can happen. You will be given a decision notice with the reasons why permission was not forthcoming. From this point you can either give up, re-apply taking the points listed into consideration, or appeal.

If your application is *delegated*, it will be referred to a senior planning officer. The planning committee will have already come to a virtual conclusion over the application but for one reason or another cannot totally commit to it. From this point the senior planning officer will await the contentious point to be resolved before giving a final verdict.

As with a delegated decision, a contentious issue or the late arrival of certain documentation could hold up an application. However, if the committee wishes to make the final decision, rather than pass it on to a planning officer, the matter will be *deferred* until a later date.

If *permission is granted*, make sure you read any conditions carefully. If you find these too strict, or are refused permission all together, you can appeal to the Secretary of State or re-apply with a different design.

The vagaries of planning departments can cause frustrations, but understanding what goes into a planning decision is vital for your success.

VAT

The labour and materials used in a self-build project are all free of VAT. Any VAT-registered contractors should not include VAT in their bills and, if you are managing your own site, you can claim back any VAT you pay within three months of the building being completed. Send in all invoices and receipts to Customs & Excise and the refund will be sent out within weeks.

smart move

a range of mortgages to make yourself a home

please call into your nearest branch

MORTGAGES WORTH TALKING ABOUT

Lloyds TSB
Scotland

Building yourself a future
Self build mortgage advice on your doorstep

When you go househunting, you're faced with the fact that you're going to have to make compromises. Unless you're very fortunate, you'll probably have to balance the location, facilities and features you want against the budget you have available. But there's no alternative, is there? Well, you could always embark on a self-build, conversion or renovation project. It's a lot to take on and needs serious consideration, but if you know exactly what you want, self-building could be the way to get it.

Mortgage advice on your doorstep
Of course, financing a construction project can be tricky and you'll need expert help, but you don't necessarily need to have a huge amount of money available initially – there are specialist mortgages that can help you right from the start, when you buy the land or the building to renovate. So with a growing number of self-build mortgages on the market, how do you choose between them to find the one that's right for you?

Thankfully, at any branch of Lloyds TSB Scotland you can talk to a mortgage arranger who can give you guidance. You can also pick up lots of literature to read in your own time to help you decide what options are best for you. In fact, you can get almost everything you need to build (or buy) a home at Lloyds TSB Scotland – a mortgage, a repayment method and even insurance that's tailored to meet your project's individual needs (such as site insurance and public liability cover).

Building yourself a future
There are two main stumbling blocks with self-building: first, finding the initial lump of money to buy either the land to build on or the building to renovate or convert and secondly, keeping the cash flowing

so you can pay for work without the stress of working in arrears. When you're looking for a mortgage lender, it's important to bear these points in mind and find out how much help you're offered.

It's important to check what percentage of the cost of the land your lender will cover. Some will only offer 50 or 60%, leaving you to find the rest of the initial outlay – which can be serious when you consider that the price of the land can be up to 40% of the total build cost. However, there are lenders out there who will lend up to 95% of the land and building costs, making self-building a real possibility for all kinds of people, even those without a massive nest-egg.

Experienced self-build lenders appreciate the difficulties and will offer you 'stage payments', splitting the money up into chunks for a steady flow of cash throughout your build. Another big plus is a lender who gives you a dedicated expert contact on their team who can give you help and advice throughout your project.

Check the whole package

Finally, look out for special offers and check what's included in the mortgages you are comparing. While one lender may offer you a low rate, they may charge fees such as MIG – the Mortgage Indemnity Guarantee, also known as the Lender's Risk Fee. This is a payment that insures the lender against the risk of a borrower defaulting on their mortgage and it can add several hundred pounds to your costs. Lloyds TSB Scotland, which offers loans to buy homes in Scotland, has abolished MIG fees on all their mortgages. For more information on the full range of Lloyds TSB Scotland mortgages, which includes discount rate, tracker, cash gift and fixed rate mortgages as well as self-build mortgages, call into any branch and talk to a mortgage arranger about making yourself a home.

Lloyds TSB Scotland mortgages: for important information please refer to the advertisement overleaf.

THE NATIONAL FEDERATION OF
ROOFING CONTRACTORS (NFRC)

The National Federation of Roofing Contractors (NFRC) (0207 436 0387) is the largest roofing trade association in the UK whose members include some 750 contractor companies and 118 manufacturers and service providers. Every contractor member is carefully vetted to ensure that they comply with the NFRC's Code of Practice, are suitably qualified to lay products to specification, have sound Health and Safety policies in place and are covered by third party and public liability insurance.

The Federation has a variety of tailor-made insurance packages which members can offer to the clients, since investing in independent insurance is an important consideration when thinking about getting any kind of construction work done. These independent guarantees give the client added peace of mind for up to 10 years for domestic work and 15 years for commercial work. A typical domestic insurance guarantee costs £20 for the whole 10 years.

You can also get free and help and advice in the unlikely event of any disputes between you and your contractor or make use of the NFRC's technical advisory service.

To get a free list of NFRC registered member contractors in your area visit the website at www.nfrc.co.uk or call 0207 436 0387. So if you find yourself in any doubt over who to trust, remember that the NFRC have already done the checking for you!

10

Making extra money from your existing property

Increase your mortgage

The most obvious way to raise cash from your home is to take a lump sum by increasing your mortgage. This is also called a 'further advance.' You'll have to repay at your lender's standard variable rate, but as the cheapest personal loan rates are at least two or three per cent higher, you should save money.

A loan from a High Street bank costs more like 14 per cent APR. An additional loan is only worth having if your property is worth a lot more than the mortgage outstanding.

If you think you might want to take a slice of cash more than once, then think about a flexible or current account loan. With most flexible and current account plans you can take the money out of your account (up to a pre-set borrowing limit) without asking permission.

The independent statistics magazine *Moneyfacts* (*www.moneyfacts.co.uk*) has a selection of the best rates for flexible loans and personal loans.

Most lenders are amenable to giving extra loans, but it isn't widely publicised. All you need to do is phone your lender, ask what the process is, and you should be on your way.

You will have to pay for a current market valuation on your home (take this fee into account when weighing up the cost of an additional loan against a cheap personal loan). There may also be an arrangement fee.

You can choose to repay over a fixed period – either a shorter period of three or five years or as long as the mortgage – and the additional loan is kept separate from the rest of your mortgage borrowing.

Renovate your house

By planning any refurbishment or alterations carefully it is possible to increase your profit when you sell.

Firstly, there are a number of ways you can improve your property so that it saves you money. New building regulations mean homes are to become more energy efficient. Replacement windows should be double-glazed, boilers must be energy efficient, and conservatories and extensions better insulated. Improvements like these mean utility bills should be lower.

If your plans are more dramatic, remember the best way of substantially increasing the value of your home is by increasing its space and size. Adding an extra bedroom, an en suite bathroom, a large kitchen-diner, family room or conservatory will invariably increase the value of your home.

Always check if you need planning permission and building regulations approval. Keep all the relevant paperwork.

Equity release schemes

This kind of scheme is often of interest to older homeowners who are 'asset rich but cash poor.' Their house – usually with little or no mortgage on it – is mortgaged to raise a loan, which is used to purchase a pension, which is then used to supplement the borrower's income. The loan is also used to pay back interest on the sum borrowed. Be careful – this can be an expensive way to obtain extra money. If interest rates go up, the cost of servicing the loan would also rise and could take the majority of the income raised to pay back. Choose any scheme carefully and consider how flexible it is. Find a lender who operates under the Safe

Home Income Plan scheme (SHIP) and always take advice from an independent advisor.

Location, location, location – cut!

You could make several hundred pounds a day if your home is used as a location for film or TV. All sorts of homes can appeal, and in some areas (especially in cities) you may find you get requests from location scouts posted through your door.

If you use an agency to market your home as a location, it will take a fee from any earnings you make, usually 10–15 per cent (plus VAT). For example, you can see what sorts of home are already on offer, and register online with the Location Partnership (*www.locationpartnership.com*) or Lavish Locations (*www.lavishlocations.co.uk*).

The BBC also runs a location register. You will be asked for photos and details of your home and will have to fill in a questionnaire (call 020 8225 9133).

Rent a room

Renting out a spare room is the most traditional way to make extra money. Many years ago the Government brought in incentives for this, under the Rent-a-Room scheme. If the income from your lodger is £4,250 or less, there's no tax to pay.

A Monday to Friday rental might be a good idea if you live in a city: people working away from home often need temporary lodging. All the better if your spare room has an en suite bathroom. Check out the going rate for room rentals in the local press.

Language schools are often in need of hosts for their students, although you may need to cook food and offer some pastoral care in exchange for the extra income. Then there are festivals and sporting events. Temporary accommodation is always needed, so you could move out for the duration and make some serious cash.

House swapping

This is increasingly popular especially as the Internet has enabled it to take off in a big way. It's not so much about making money from your property as more of a way of saving on holiday expenses. You simply swap homes with someone else for a holiday – or longer as some swaps last several months and would suit retired people looking for a long break.

Online directories list homeowners in other countries and details of their homes and available swapping dates. You can respond to these advertisements and/or advertise your own place and the places you'd like to visit. There's the additional benefit of leaving your house occupied while you are away, but you'll need to be relaxed about other people being in your home – and even driving your car.

Try www.homebase-hols.com or www.homexchange.com.

11

Improving your home

It may be stating the obvious, but if you don't like something about your property – change it. You don't have to live with someone else's decorating style or taste when you own your own home, so take advantage of the freedom and make it suit you.

Get rid of the swirly purple-patterned carpet, brighten up the kitchen, lose the dated avocado bathroom suite. Unless it's a major extension you're planning, you don't have to ask anyone's permission, it's your taste, your lifestyle and what you want that counts.

Of course, the amount of money you have will play a part in the creation of your dream home. If you have thousands of pounds, there's no doubt you can spend them. A top-of-the-range kitchen is in the £20,000-plus bracket. At the other end of the scale, £20 on a tin of white paint and some free hard work and enthusiasm – yours – smartens up a scruffy hallway.

If you can bear to, and it's practical, it's always a good idea to live in a house first before you plan any major changes. After a few weeks you know which rooms get the morning light and which benefit in the evening. If the sun shines so strongly into your bedroom it wakens you at dawn, then darker curtains are a must, and that will obviously affect any colour choice when it comes to decorating.

You will find out what items of furniture fit best into a particular space, which pieces you do really need to keep and which are now surplus to requirements. Put a couple of penny ads in the local paper and sell off what you don't want – put the cash back into your Dream Home Fund.

The basics

Don't do even the simplest job until you've had a chance to really think about the basics. What's the point of putting a set of shelves up on an internal wall when putting them in the alcoves would provide some cheap soundproofing from next-door's children? And no good will come of ripping out those old cupboards if a) they cover a spaghetti junction of pipes and b) you need the storage.

Look at the layout of the house. Is the best use being made of the space? Is that small room, which barely fits a single bed, not better fitted out with a desk and chair and used as a study?

Should the utility room be downstairs? What's the point of carrying clothes downstairs to be washed and ironed and then up again? Can't you move the room and have more living space on the ground floor?

Would knocking down an internal wall bring a lot more light into a room, or is it better to have a larger kitchen-diner than a separate kitchen and under-used dining room?

Kitchens and bathrooms are the two rooms that can cause problems. They cost a lot of money to replace and, perhaps because they are the most used rooms in the house, it can be very difficult to decide what is the best way forward. This is when it's essential to ask for expert advice. If you want a power shower, you need to find out about the water pressure. Before you buy that trendy and expensive cooker, you need to find out if the extractor fan can be fitted on an inside wall.

Major renovations

If you want to build an extension, add a conservatory, or do a loft conversion, then the advice of an architect or experienced builder, is a must.

You may think such a large building project would be too expensive or too much trouble, and moving into a new home would be a better idea. But extending upwards or outwards is much, much cheaper than estate agents' commission, stamp duty, removal costs and legal fees.

Stamp duty, in particular, is a killer. Payable by the buyer, it's a tax on already taxed income, and at one per cent for properties under £250,000, moving up to three per cent for properties over that figure but under £500,000, it can amount to a bill of thousands of pounds for simply changing your address.

So as good conversions always add value to your home and you will recoup your investment when you sell, you may want to hand a cheque over to the builder rather than the Chancellor of the Exchequer – you stand more chance of getting a return on your investment.

Improving your home, whether for yourself and family to live in or to make it easier to sell, can be a fraught process as mistakes can be costly to put right. But if you get expert advice, collect estimates for any work, have a good idea of what you want and, most importantly, take your time, you will find the challenge of it fun and satisfying.

Hallways

The first impression of your home should be welcoming. If the passageway is dark, choose a lighter shade of paint, install a couple of bright bulbs in the lights and hang a couple of carefully placed mirrors to reflect the light. Paint the radiator the same colour as the wall or hide it with a smart cover. Consider what would be the right kind of flooring. Wood or tiles are usually best for such a high traffic area. If you want a carpet ask at the showroom for a hard-wearing type, woven to withstand the wear and tear of football boots, trainers, wellingtons, work boots and gardening shoes. If there's space for a coat cupboard and other clutter, fit one, if not buy strong wall hooks and perhaps a shoe rack to keep everything tidy.

The sitting room

One person's good taste is another's example of 'naffness'. But you can't decorate for others, it's important that you live in a place that's comfortable and suits you and the way you live. It helps though if you don't have to do a complete makeover when you come to sell. Here's a basic guideline to help you overcome any pitfalls.

Focus on the space. Visualise the room as you want it. Think about where you will put electrical appliances like the CD player, the TV and lamps because all the wiring and cabling should be done before any decorating. The same goes for radiators. If you are installing a new central heating system, plan carefully to put the radiators in the most convenient places. Also, it's worth considering fitting under-floor heating. It's not so expensive anymore, is reasonable to run and is much more convenient when you come to place the furniture.

Remember that rooms always look smaller when empty so think about the sizes of furniture and fixtures carefully. A useful interior designer tip is always to buy a size larger than you think you need. So choose a larger lampshade, a bigger chair, and a chunkier coffee table.

Flooring and carpets

Flooring is all-important for comfort and warmth. If you decide on wooden flooring, you may need new floorboards or can sand and varnish the originals. If you have to fit new, think about installing a sound insulation strip underneath, especially if you live above others or in an upstairs room. Laminate flooring can look as good as the real thing and is cheap and easy to fit. If the floorboards are already in good shape, you can hire a sander and do at least a couple of rooms in one day.

If you think carpet is more comfortable, always buy the best you can afford – it's a false economy to skimp here – and, thinking ahead to selling, choose a plain rather than a patterned design.

Another interior design tip is to use the same carpet, tiles or wooden flooring throughout the house. This trick offers an illusion of space as spaces seem to flow seamlessly into one another and it's easier on the eye.

Original tiled or stone floors are worth keeping as a 'feature'.

LOOK FOR THE BUTTERFLY

& PRADO CARPETS
EST 1908

YOUR ASSURANCE OF HIGH QUALITY CARPETS

Associated Weavers is an established company and has gained a reputation over the last thirty years for leading the tufted carpet industry. This has been achieved by using the latest technology in yarns, stain protection systems and machinery. Continual investment has ensured that our customers always have the most innovative designs, choice of colours and styles that guarantee quality whenever you buy an Associated Weavers carpet. We are the leading carpet manufacturer in Europe and have over the years been dealing with the most successful and reliable retailers, who can be found in any High Street or Retail Park.

ASSOCIATED WEAVERS

USING FUTURE TECHNOLOGY FOR CARPET TODAY

Fletchers Mill, P.O. Box 17, Dean Clough Industrial Park, Halifax, West Yorkshire, HX3 5AW.
Telephone: 01422 431100 Facsimile: 01422 431105

Module

GROUP

Delivering Choice, Performance and Style in Quality Carpet

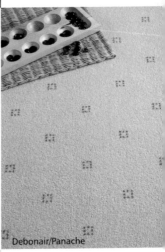
Debonair/Panache

Grampian

BALSAN

PRADO CARPETS
EST 1908

Fletchers Mill, P.O. Box 17,
Dean Clough Industrial Park,
Halifax, West Yorkshire, HX3 5AW.
Telephone: 01422 431100
Facsimile: 01422 431105

BHK CORNER THE MARKET IN LAMINATES

NEXT TIME you are looking to move or buy a new house, take a careful look at the quality of its flooring. Most houses are nowadays fitted with some form of laminate flooring, but, on closer inspection, you will see gaps in the joints and areas where the beading doesn't match the flooring properly. There will also be problems with the fittings around doorways and fireplaces, and a host of other niggling problems that point to poor installation and finishing.

Laminates specialists BHK recognised this problem was widespread in the home improvements industry, and decided immediate action was needed to correct it and produced a range of state-of-the-art laminate flooring products that made fitting problems a thing of the past. And owing to the historic lack of technical support for distributors' customers, the directors of the company decided to set a new trading pattern and sell direct to the end user.

Though initially perceived as a huge investment gamble, BHK's decision to open ten of its own showroom outlets, and to fully train their staff in all aspects of laminates has definitely paid off. BHK (UK) Ltd was recently rewarded for their professional approach to marketing their products when they won the Retail Floors Industry Award 2002 for being the best laminate supplier of the year.

BHK's success is driven by the daily contact their staff maintain with their customers, and the prices they offer. While their competitors simply sell to distributors and provide minimal technical backup, BHK's staff are fully trained and ready to answer customer questions immediately. Added to this is the fact that BHK's streamlined communications channels mean that they can react immediately to changes in demand in their manufacturing process, and requests for special orders.

When the market for laminates changed in 2001 from glued to glue-less systems, BHK's, responsiveness paid big dividends. Reacting to a change in demand, they responded with new products immediately. By using a licence to manufacture the Uniclic® system whereby laminate boards can be simply clicked together, they soon had two production lines set up producing a superb new range of flooring.

BHK are well on the way to cornering the market in laminate flooring systems, and have ten branches in the UK from Sterling in Scotland to Reading in the South of England. They also have a central warehouse in Hull that provides a cost effective method of receiving laminates in from Germany on the ferry.

BHK have become successful because they offer what the market demands, and respond to it quickly with new products. Added to this is their dedication to offering personal customer service that is delivered from economical secondary sites on the fringes of towns and cities.

Their market research shows that 80% of their custom comes from second time buyers, and word-of-mouth recommendations, and, as the end of 2002 approaches, they are due to post record sales and profit figures.

The Industry's 2002
Award Winning
Laminate Flooring

What more do we need to say?

MODERNA® LIGNO
Laminate Tiling

NEW MODERNA® TOLEDO
Cork Flooring

NEW MODERNA® LIGNO
Wood Veneer

THE WHYS AND HOWS OF BUYING YOUR SEWING MACHINE

Buying and Selling Property discovers how a small investment in a Singer Sewing Machine can seriously improve the value of your property ... and leave you with a new hobby as well!

The inside look and feel of a home makes all the difference both to those who live there and to any prospective buyer so any effort put into interior decoration pays big dividends. There is no easier way to do this than by enhancing your soft-furnishings – and what's more, you can do it yourself. We believe the place to start is your local Singer Sewing Centre.

Singer is synonymous with sewing, having pioneered the industry over 150 years ago. They still sell more machines than anyone else world-wide and offer the best value and quality for simple but effective home sewing.

The national network of Singer Sewing Centres offer friendly advice and assistance. They can explain the different aspects of a sewing machine and recommend and demonstrate the model that's right for you. They will also give you full after-sales service and support – essential for beginners and experts alike, and can provide you with all your accessories and supplies.

Once you get your machine home, we suggest you start with curtains. With an unlimited choice of excellent value fabrics available, just measure up and sew. You'll be amazed at the difference it can make to a room. Then add some cushion covers and a throw for your sofa and your home will be transformed.

But one note of caution, sewing is an enticing pastime. Before you know it you'll be bitten by the bug and be making your own designer clothes or joining your local quilting circle. Whatever may happen we wish you good sewing!

SINGER

the world's number 1 in sewing

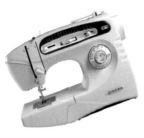  

Just call into your local Singer Sewing Centre and discover how simple sewing can be.

SINGER SEWING CENTRES:

EAST ANGLIA
Exchange St, Attleborough. Tel: 01953 454471
91 St Johns St, Bury St Edmunds. Tel: 01284 754378
22 High Street, Huntingdon. Tel: 01480 453752
8 Tower Street, Kings Lynn. Tel: 01553 773362
4 Suffolk Rd, Lowestoft. Tel: 01502 573813

MIDLANDS
2a Luke St, Bedford. Tel: 01234 350186
133 High Rd, Beeston. Tel: 01159 223904
67 Corporation St, Coventry. Tel: 02476 555282
3 Watergate, Grantham. Tel: 01476 563891
12 Widmarsh Street, Hereford. Tel: 01432 358986
43 Gold St, Northampton. Tel: 01604 637810
113 Abbey St, Nuneaton. Tel: 02476 383295

NORTH
252-6 Freeman Street, Grimsby. Tel: 01472 342334
4a Commercial Street, Harrogate. Tel: 01423 503767
30 Church Street, Keighley. Tel: 01535 662227
92 Kirkgate, Leeds. Tel: 0113 2453156
19 The Springs, Wakefield. Tel: 01924 374471
41 Fossgate, York. Tel: 01904 623403

NORTH EAST
96 Bondgate, Darlington. Tel: 01325 463630
126 Park View, Whitley Bay. Tel: 0191 2525825

NORTH WEST
108 George St, Altincham. Tel: 0161 9282485
12 Princes Pvmnt, Grange Prcnt, Birkenhead. Tel: 0151 6478040
14 Rosemary Lane, Carlisle. Tel: 01228 522758
141 Brook Street, Chester. Tel: 01244 347819
12 Chestergate, Macclesfield. Tel: 01625 424 646
67 London Street, Southport. Tel: 01704 534688
10 Vernon Street, Stockport. Tel: 0161 480 4059

SOUTH
20a St Thomas Sq, Newport, Isle of Wight. Tel: 01983 529696
18 Whitefield Rd, New Milton. Tel: 01425 620170
113 East Street, Southampton. Tel: 0238 022 4700

SOUTH EAST/LONDON
78 New London Rd, Chelmsford. Tel: 01245 354537
94 Church St, Croydon. Tel: 020 8688 1128
59 Green St, Gillingham. Tel: 01634 570254
14 Chapel Street, Guildford. Tel: 01483 575896
40 High Street, Hounslow. Tel: 020 8570 0867
60 Fife Road, Kingston. Tel: 020 8546 1828
30 Well Hall Rd, Eltham, London. Tel: 020 8859 0303
666-668 High Rd, N. Finchley, London. Tel: 020 8446 5118
152 Fortress Rd, Kentish Town, London. Tel: 020 7485 1653
3 Chigwell Rd, South Woodford, London. Tel: 020 8989 0686
38 Thomas St, Woolwich, London. Tel: 020 8854 0124
262 High St, Orpington. Tel: 01689 828195
42 York Road, Southend-on-Sea. Tel: 01702 347316
4 High Street, Southall. Tel: 020 8574 1750
1 West Blk, Embassy Crt, High St, Welling. Tel: 020 8304 0869
41 Chertsey Rd, Woking. Tel: 01483 773595

SOUTH WEST
7 St Nicholas Street, Bodmin. Tel: 01208 72166
14 Castle Gallery, Broadmead, Bristol. Tel: 0117 9264071
Spread Eagle Crt, 110 Northgate, Gloucester. Tel: 01452 506509
60 Torquay Rd, Paignton. Tel: 01803 556692
2 Queen St, Penzance. Tel: 01736 363 457
11 John Street, Truro. Tel: 01872 225168

NORTHERN IRELAND
23 Wellington St, Ballymena. Tel: 028256 40034
14 Donegall Rd, Belfast. Tel: 02890 326002

SCOTLAND
199-201 Balgreen Rd, Edinburgh. Tel: 0131 346 0990
U 58 Savoy Ctr, Sauchiehall St, Glasgow. Tel: 0141 332 4318
130 West Blackhall St, Greenock. Tel: 01475 724162
71 Causeyside St, Paisley. Tel: 0141 887 9944

WALES
17/18 The Market, Carmarthen. Tel: 01267 220808
2 The Market, Llanelli. Tel: 01554 774623
31 Taff St, Pontypridd. Tel: 01443 492 828
4 Market Street, Rhyl. Tel: 01745 351175

Your guide to quality and reliability

Founded in 1947 the Association of Master Upholsterers is arguably one of the oldest trade associations' involved in the furniture industry. Every prospective member of the Association is evaluated personally by a senior Association assessor prior to acceptance, this ensures only the best are recruited.

We have a member that can cater to your requirements, whether they be Curtains and Loose Covers, Re-upholstery or brand new Custom made suites or chairs. Members' are all genuine businesses who are well versed in current Fire & Safety legislation which relates to furniture, and all use the very best of available materials.

Inviting an AMU Member to call to discuss your furnishing requirements, is to unveil a plethora of choice. With literally thousands of fabrics and combinations available to choose from, you will find yourself guided skilfully through the complexities by an expert with years of experience in the craft.

For further information about the Association, its aims and objectives, or to find a member in your area, please see the website or call us **(01633) 215454**.

Web: www.upholsterers.co.uk   E-mail: info@upholsterers.co.uk

What are you doing this weekend?

Spending time with your family and friends or doing the decorating?

We're sure decorating is the last thing you want to be doing but finding a quality decorator to take over the job can be a minefield.

That's where the **Dulux Select Decorator Service** comes in. Our free service is nationwide and recommends approved decorators in your area. Because we've assessed them on the quality of their work, you can be sure that they'll do a good job – we even offer a 12 month guarantee on all workmanship and materials when **Dulux Trade** products have been used.

Plus research shows **Dulux Select Decorators** have 29% more 'completely satisfied' customers than those recommended from another source and customers are 25% more likely to recommend them to their friends.

So now you can forget the worries of hiring a decorator... and this weekend concentrate on having a good time.

The **Dulux Select Decorator Service** – Quality Decorators from a Brand you can trust.

For your nearest **Dulux Select Decorator** call us on: 0845 76 97 668 or email us via our web site www.duluxdecorator.co.uk

Finding a decorator can be a battlefield, with a huge number of considerations and associated worry. How can you be sure that you've chosen a decorator capable of high quality work, that will treat your home and belongings with respect? Will your deposit be safe? Will the best quality materials be used, and what happens if you're not happy with the work?

Imagine being assured of all those worries before you even pick up the phone. The Dulux Select Decorator Service exists to make choosing a decorator as hassle and risk-free as possible.

The service is free and recommends decorators in your area from a national network of approved decorators that have been quality assessed by Dulux and are governed by a Code of Conduct. Because Dulux has assessed their work they seem pretty confident that they'll do a good job and offer a 12-month guarantee on all workmanship and materials when Dulux Trade products have been used. A £2 million public liability insurance ensures that even if there is an accident your belongings are covered – and don't worry about any deposit – that's safeguarded aswell.

Free recommendations can be requested by phoning 0845 769 7668 or visiting www.duluxdecorator.co.uk. You will receive details of decorators in your area for you to contact at your own convenience, together with a copy of Dulux's customer guarantee form and a Dulux colour card to assist you in your colour choices. Then its over to you – 'no salesman will call'!

Many of the Dulux decorators will not only quote for the work, but can also assist with colour choice and scheming. Using MousePainter™, the revolutionary colour scheming tool from Dulux, that allows you to visualize your colour ideas on screen using a number of different roomsets that you can 'paint' by clicking on different options from the latest Dulux ranges.

If the shade you want isn't available you can obtain any colour using the Advanced Eye for Colour system. Just supply your decorator with a sample and they can have it scanned to the colour you desire.

Once you've agreed your price and the decorator sets to work you can feel fairly assured that a good job is being done.

Research shows Dulux Decorators have 29% more 'completely satisfied' customers than those recommended from another source and they are 25% more likely to recommend them to their friends. Yvonne Morley from Hampton commented "My neighbours, family, friends, work colleagues and local community in general are impressed by the standards set."

Once the work is finished Dulux asks that a customer guarantee form is completed and returned to them to validate your guarantee. There's also a section to rate your decorator on a number of attributes, so Dulux can monitor the performance of their members and assure that the standard is kept at a premium.

In the unlikely event you are unhappy with the quality of the job, the Select customer service team is on hand to deal with any complaints. An assessor will be sent out to inspect the work and if it is found to be below standard all necessary steps will be taken to make amends.

Dulux has covered all angles when it comes to the problems and pitfalls of hiring a decorator by supplying a no-nonsense, value-for-money and completely reliable home decorating service that provides the customer with a level of control – from the initial referral period right through to a supported mechanism for customer complaint.

Call **0845 769 7668** or visit www.duluxdecorator.co.uk

Decorating

When it comes to decorating, less is more. Don't use lots of matching borders, wallpapers, curtains, cushions and throws. You can now even get matching wastepaper baskets in some designs! And don't paper all four walls with a very 'busy' theme. Put the expensive patterned paper on one wall and use a plainer design or plain paper on the others.

Pale colours can still be warming, yet they open a room up more and sell a property more quickly than dark colours. There's room for a little drama, particularly in the dining room, where the English seem to favour crimson.

White ceilings make them appear higher; dark colours lower them. And woodwork should be white or off-white. Painting walls white, however, won't necessarily make the room appear lighter. Use the mirror trick for that, and place a selection of table and standard lamps around the room to light up any dark corners.

Experimenting with different paint colours and effects is one of the cheapest ways to change a look and is easily changed if the colour doesn't look good.

Windows and doors

Replacing windows and doors can be expensive if you want to install double-glazing throughout or as cheap as chips if all you need to do is to re-hang a badly fitted and situated door. Of course, double-glazing is a major investment, but you usually get your money back when you come to sell and the savings on heating bills are worth making especially if you are in the property for a long time. If your home is in a conservation area, you must check before buying the property or installation if uPVC windows are acceptable.

When it comes to doors, think about the style and age of the property and the room. Is the room a little dark? Have a door with glass panels. Is the house an Edwardian Villa-style? Consider getting a couple of stained-

Window Shopping

The good news is that windows have largely become far more sophisticated in design during recent years. And let's be frank, they had to begin matching customers' expectations pretty quickly. For long gone are the days when all window companies appeared the same. A few have grabbed the opportunity to offer higher quality as consumers expect more for their money. In today's market place however, the choices seem endless to the untrained eye so more than ever it pays to shop around.

So what should you be looking for and how much can you expect to pay?

To help, let's start with the three main reasons for deciding on windows. The first is based on aesthetics. How good do the windows actually look? This is probably more important than you think because people notice windows when they're bad. So if you go down market, beware of affecting the saleability of your home. It's always best to avoid thick, plastic-looking frames. Insist on equal sight lines (where the opening and non-opening windows are the same size) – most people don't, and it looks horrible.

The second reason for choosing one product over another is security. Far too many window companies use externally beaded glass. This is where the pane can be removed from outside the property without entering it. Why anyone would want to risk being broken into like this is beyond comprehension. Yet, hundreds of thousands of windows are being sold today that invite intruders. The security should also extend to a multi-point locking system, claw hooks that grasp the opening firmly into the frame and a shoot-bolt system so the windows cannot be levered out from the top or bottom. Remember, with a home broken into every 90 seconds, potential thieves are looking for the easy option.

Finally, technology plays a huge factor in which windows to choose. There are some amazing developments in the industry concerning glass that will make living in the property an absolute pleasure. Insist on low-emissivity glass such as Pilkington K and sealed units filled with Argon gas. *The reason?* You'll save about 30% on your heating bill for a start as these types of sealed unit act like an insulating blanket. Remarkably, the glass lets in the warmth of the Sun but bounces back heat from radiators. You'll also ensure that you're not breaking the law as these far exceed the new Government regulations on heat loss through windows.

So what should you expect to pay? Well the rule of thumb has recently been about 10% of the property value. However, as house prices increase, this figure falls because window prices rarely rise as fast as property. As a guide, you really shouldn't look to invest less than 5% of the property value on windows. The reality is you'd probably consider between 7.5% to 10% to ensure the quality. So on a typical £100,000 home, £7,500 might be a mid-point.

You honestly do get what you pay for with windows. It's probably one area of investment in your property that you should never skimp on. The message is get the best windows you can afford, not the cheapest you can get. That's because you'll be unlikely to see a negative return on investment if you do. One of the few ways to lose out is by falling in to the trap of installing low quality products into an appreciating asset such as a property. When it comes to sell your property, a prospective buyer could use the fact that inferior windows might need replacing and detract from the value, potentially knocking thousands off the asking price. So take your time and get it right first time.

HOME SOLUTIONS FROM STANLEY SLIDING DOORS

Providing a complete, co-ordinated finish while maximising precious space, Stanley's Sliding Doors collection offers the perfect home storage solution.

CHILD'S PLAY

The line 'tidy your bedroom' is all well and good, unless you have piles of toys and limited space under your bed. The perfect solution comes in the shape of Stanley Sliding Doors funky kids' collection.

TRANSFORM YOUR WORKSPACE

Stanley's stylish Home Office collection is perfect for keeping track of finances and filing away important documents.

Perfect for clearing away clutter. The functional yet stylish range reflects the latest interior looks and incorporates mirrored, frosted, coloured and wood effect doors. Co-ordinating shelving and drawers are perfect for organising everything from clothes to toys to paperwork.

Stanley Sliding Doors are available from all major retailers including Homebase and B&Q with prices starting from around £57.99 per door.

Stylish & Fashionable ☑   Great Value ☑

Maximum Storage ☑   Easy-to-install ☑

**For more details contact
Stanley Sliding Doors Customer Services on 0114 276 4099**

STANLEY
HomeSolutions

THE PERFECT FINISH STARTS WITH STANLEY

For a fresh new look that boasts lasting appeal, simply follow Stanley's seven top tips to decorating success.

Stanley's top tips:

1 Carpets are vulnerable to unwanted spillages from pots of paint, wallpaper paste and even cups of tea. Priced from around £1.50, Stanley's Dust Sheets are guaranteed to get it covered!

2 Stanley's Carpet Shield on a roll is priced around £5.60 for 12m and comprises of creased strips that can be cut to fit, making it ideal for protecting carpets when painting skirting boards.

For more information contact Stanley Customer Services on 01422 832089.

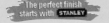

3 For best results buy a good brush and work on a rough wall to knock out loose fillings before painting. The Stanley Premier Brush range, priced around £5 for a 2" brush, will give good results and long service.

4 If you have awkward areas that need painting, Stanley's Long Handled Roller, priced from around £6.30, is ideal for getting behind radiators, in between beams and around high windows.

5 Rollers are great for getting the job done, but flying drops can be a hazard! Some rollers come complete with a shield to ensure the paint only goes where you want. Stanley Roller & Shield is priced around £5.50.

6 Paint Pads are perfect for creating clean, smooth lines and for picking up and releasing paint easily without creating air bubbles or leaving visible brush strokes. As pictured, Stanley's Flock Paint Pad Set is priced from around £7.76.

7 Offering colour, texture and warmth all rolled into one, it's no surprise that wallpaper is making a massive comeback. Pictured here, Stanley's Wallpapering Kit which includes a seam roller, a paste brush and paperhanging brush, plumb bob and line, wallpaper edger and a pair of scissors, is priced from around £20.

TEMPTED TO TRY OUT THE TOP TIPS FOR YOURSELF?

To check out Stanley's extensive selection of decorating products simply pop along to your nearest DIY retailer including Homebase and B&Q.

glass doors. Is the room going to be used as a teenager's den? You'll need a heavy, well-fitted door to keep the noise of any music in.

Have a look at the layout of the room and see if the door is better opening on the other side. Does that give more room or better access?

The dining room

In many homes the dining room is the least used of any room in the house. 'Do you really need it?' should be the question you ask. It's all down to lifestyle and, practically, whether or not the kitchen is big enough to eat in. Many people now have the best of both worlds by knocking through, if possible, an adjoining wall and having one large kitchen-diner. That's all very well if you don't mind having a dinner party and your guests eat surrounded by evidence of the chaos that has gone into the cooking and the detritus of the meal at its end. But if you only have close friends and family around and you would rather put the room to better use as a second sitting room, or a children's playroom, you can because it's your house!

The kitchen

This is an important room and it's pretty crucial to get any renovation done properly as, when you do come to sell, a kitchen can make or break a sale, and to correct or change anything then can be expensive.

Sorting out a budget is the first thing to do. It doesn't matter what kind of kitchen you want, most styles can be found to suit any price range, but there's no point shooting off to a designer store if you don't have the money, nor traipsing off to a discount warehouse if you don't want a flatpack.

The whole process was a pleasure, because those Magnet people obviously live, eat and breathe fitted kitchens.

STUDIO OAK

At Magnet, our enthusiasm for improving your home is obvious from the second you walk through our door. Our sales people know our ranges inside out. Our designers thrive on bringing your ideas together in the form of a 3D colour plan. We'll even organise a home visit just to iron out any potential problems. Then it's all systems go to installation and, before you know it, we'll be arranging an after sales visit to make sure you're totally happy with the job.

Call **0845 123 6789** for details of your nearest showroom quoting code B+SP or visit **www.magnet.co.uk**

Magnet a pleasure for life

Design Your Dream Kitchen with Magnet

'If you've just moved house and you're not keen on the kitchen that you have inherited, then look no further than your local Magnet store for help in designing your dream kitchen.

Choosing a new kitchen is a big task, but it should be an enjoyable one. It gives you the chance to create something that is totally unique and totally yours. Magnet offers everything you need to create your perfect kitchen from its extensive range of units, to its fantastic range of kitchen appliances and planning and installation expertise.

When considering your new kitchen there are several key areas to think about initially. Take in to account what space is available to you and how you would ideally like to utilise it. Consider who uses your kitchen and who does the cooking. Do you use it for purposes other than cooking and are there children to consider?

Also, think about what appliances you need as they are all fundamental to the layout of a kitchen. Magnet has an extensive choice of appliances including ovens, fridges, freezers, dishwashers and washing machines from leading brands such as AEG, Zanussi, Neff, Die Dietrich and Whirlpool. Once you have assessed your basic requirements, you can then move on to the exciting bits!

Now is the time to think about what style of kitchen you want and the additional extras such as lighting, flooring and display details which will help you create a totally unique and individual kitchen.

When choosing the style you want, think about what sort of feel you want in the kitchen - practical and professional, contemporary, warm and homely or something more unusual?

Magnet has over 35 kitchen ranges to choose from so there is a design for every taste. For a sleek, minimalist look think about plain, flat fronted designs with stainless steel handles and accessories and units in pale tones such as white, beech or cream. Magnet's Studio and Stainless Steel kitchens provide an ultra minimalist solution.

For a more traditional look consider solid oak, pine, pale woods and pastels. Magnet's Bakersfield Timber and Shaker ranges offer the ultimate blend of design – traditional styles with a contemporary twist.

Take advantage of clever internal storage devices, which keep things off work surfaces such as pull-out larders and door shelves. Magnet offers a wide choice of worktops to complement their kitchen ranges. Choose from granite, Corian, wood or laminate to complete your kitchen's look and character.

Add the final individual touches to your kitchen with your choice of lighting, flooring and décor.

No matter what type of kitchen you want, Magnet can offer practical tips and planning expertise to help you achieve it.

Magnet's Full Circle Service gives you the ultimate service for creating, designing and installing your kitchen. They offer expert designers who will use their extensive knowledge, creativity and experience to bring your dream kitchen to life. Once your kitchen is designed they will also pay you a free home visit to check all the plans and offer a professional installation service. Then once your kitchen has been fitted your Magnet designer will pay you a home visit to ensure you're completely happy with everything.

For details of your nearest Magnet store or to request a brochure please call
0845 123 6789 *or visit* **www.magnet.co.uk**

IT ALL HAPPENS IN A PAULA ROSA KITCHEN

"In the contemporary home the kitchen is much more than just a functional cooking and eating area. It is the epicentre of the house, a social gathering place that should reflect your own individual style and taste". (Sir Terence Conran).

At Paula Rosa each kitchen is tailored made to suit note only your dreams but also your functional requirements. So, when stepping onto the property ladder the investment in a new, well designed kitchen makes sound financial sense.

Paula Rosa recently launched 4 new kitchens designs onto the market, all reflecting the latest trends in kitchen design.

Oak makes a comeback in the classically modern 'Sherwood' kitchen. Classic in concept but modern in the design due to wider framed doors (103mm). Carefully selected door furniture also gives a choice between traditional and modern designs. A superb quality finish is also maintained with absolute consistency between the frame and centre panel. The great Oak revival is here!

The 'Cologne' range takes the simple Shaker design into a new dimension. The bleached oak finish signals the continuing revival of this famous traditional wood and, combined with the ultra wide frames. All in all Cologne takes the Shaker concept into a new, refreshing area. The effective 'wedge' shaped design and styling on the door frame is a particularly individual feature. Attention has also been paid to door furniture with a choice of aluminium and metal handles giving the 'Cologne' range either a modern or more traditional feel.

The elegant new 'Alaska' kitchen is stunning in its line and simplicity. The door design features a distinctive step detail between the frame and panel. A range of aluminium knobs and handles marry perfectly with the pure white surfaces. "Alaska" has magical appeal when contrasted with strong wall and floor colours.

If your preference is for the minimalist look, the 'Oslo' kitchen is available in either a fashionable bleached oak with a horizontal grain on the doors or pure white. Both options offer a 'linear optic' effect – this being an aluminium effect frame that contrasts with the alternative finishes. The choice of knobs and handles includes a slim-line handle giving particular visual eloquence to the bleached oak finish.

A new, updated 68 page Kitchen brochure is now available from Paula Rosa showing their complete range, including the new kitchens detailed above.

Alternatively why not view these new ranges yourselves? Telephone 01903 748439 for your nearest stock list.

For further information contact:
Marketing Department
Paula Rosa
Water Lane, Storrington
West Sussex, RH20 3DS
Tel: 01903 746666 Fax: 01903 742140
Email: info@paularosa.com
www.paularosa.com

What's cookin' at Paula Rosa

Alaska

Oslo

Sherwood

Cologne

Four crackling new kitchens, for starters.

Alaska – pure, white simplicity.

Oslo – simple, minimalist design in white or bleached oak.

Sherwood – a classic, oak design with contemporary touches.

Cologne – stylish, modern design in bleached oak.

All part of an exciting new menu from Paula Rosa.

PAULA ROSA

Plan Oven (bottom right):
New cooking functions with electronic controls and a Safe Cool Touch System that keeps the door's temperature at less than 40ºC.

Plan Dishwasher (bottom left):
An A class performance.
Perfect cleaning and drying guaranteed.
Quiet operation.

Plan Hob:
5 burner gas hob with triple ring burner and flame failure device.

Plan Microwave Oven:
3 cooking options (microwave, grill, microwave plus grill).
Easy access drop down door.

Plan Cooker Hood:
An elegant design combined with powerful extraction – 4 speed settings.
Back lit with electronic controls.

The Candy Plan Range
It's impossible to spoil the effect

Kitchen Countertops as part of Designer Kitchens

'The countertop is the most important element in a kitchen, and the kitchen is the most important room in the home.' Irrefutable!!!

Most builders would agree that the plot sells the house and the kitchen makes it a home!!!!

We spend a large part of our lives in the kitchen and the countertop takes all we can throw at it.

We prepare food on it, drink from it, cook underneath it, wash up in it and the worktop is the most visible part of the kitchen.

It needs to be hygienic, easy to clean, look good and colour complement the kitchen (100) units, appliances and floors.

AND LASTLY the countertop material needs to give the designer the freedom to customise to consumers tastes and needs.

Kitchen Designers are always striving to maximise the functionality whilst maintaining the overall appeal of the kitchen.

The countertop or worktop must give the designer that ability to maximise their talents.

Up until recently Laminate tops have been the industry standard, giving a huge colour offer and a relatively long life. Consumers are continuing to spend more on their tops because their expectations of aesthetics, hygiene and longevity have grown.

Consumers have choices to make on the (200) type of finish, high gloss, matt, satin sheen etc.

Designers have a large selection of surfaces to choose from to tempt the adventurous consumer. Granite, solid surfaces, solid wood, slate, stainless steel are the most popular and growing considerably.

DuPont Surfaces now has two complementary surfaces to achieve all of the above.

Corian® achieves the highest satisfaction levels of all surfaces, research shows that over 90 % of purchasers would recommend Corian® to friends or relatives.

Corian® has a huge colour range, over 70 colours all of which are complemented by subtle 'shades of white' FULLY INTEGRATED sinks and bowls. (300) The integration of Corian® sinks in Corian® tops leaves a smooth, seamless joint and creates the ultimate in hygienic wet areas.

Corian® continues to allow designers to create sweeps and curves along the countertop; coving to allow a smooth transition from horizontal to vertical cladding, and round, oval dining areas attached to the countertop.

Accessories in Corian® makes customising tops and kitchens easier. Added features like Corian® knobs and handles, Taps from Avilion® with Corian® handles, Corian® Preparation Boards helps in adding that finishing touch to any design.

The new sensational material from DuPont is called Zodiaq®.

Made from the highest quality quartz, Zodiaq® is the most natural looking glossy surface, with unique strength, depth, clarity and radiance.

An exciting range of colours including deep reds and blues gives the design world a field (400) day to achieve stunning effects.

Exceptionally hard and cool to the touch, Zodiaq® is also non-porous, stain and heat resistant making it thoroughly hygienic and easy to maintain.

However the skills of kitchen designers these days are tested as many consumers would like to 'mix and match' several materials. Designers knowledge is also tested as they need to know ALL the features and benefits of each surface to guide consumers to the perfect countertop solution.

All these new materials are much more expensive than laminate but then again they have a lot more to offer.

Beautiful, hygienic, freedom in (500) design, easy to clean, are some of the words that can be used to justify spending larger proportions of customers budget on the countertop.

Corian® and Zodiaq® give 'value added' its true meaning as they complement not only the kitchen units, appliances and floor but their use can be expanded into other areas of the home, such as the dining area and conservatories.

There has never been a time like now when there is so much choice in design and materials to make kitchens the investment of a lifetime.

FreePhone No's: UK **0800 962116**
Ireland **1800 553252**

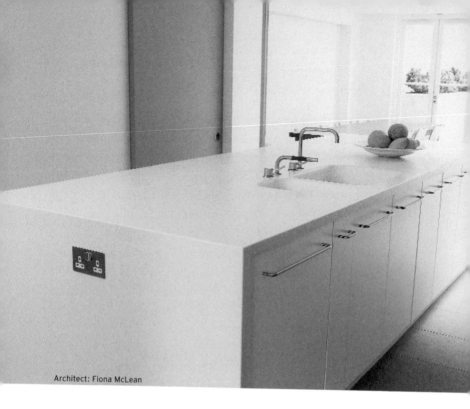

Architect: Fiona McLean

Corian®. Clean lines. Pure white.

Straight or curved, monochrome or colourful. With Corian®, you can express yourself, whichever way your tastes lean. Because Corian® can be shaped into virtually any design you can imagine. Or mixed with any other material you can think of. With over 70 striking colours to choose from, your imagination can run free. With its non-porous surfaces and seamless joints, dirts and germs will have nowhere to hide. And because Corian® is durable and renewable, the worksurface you create today will stay beautiful for years. (That should give you plenty of time to design a bathroom with Corian®.) Corian® - for all the worksurfaces in your home.

**Visit us on www.corian.co.uk or call
800/962116 (UK), 1800/553252 (IRL).**

Designer kitchens

Financially the sky's the limit with a designer kitchen. Experienced cabinetmakers can design and fit a range of solid wood units complete with granite worktops and every appliance going. You pay for their craftsmanship – a £30,000 kitchen really should last you a lifetime; their professionalism – for that kind of money you should get good service; and their imagination – most good kitchen design ideas come from the top end of the market.

The kind of companies which offer these kind of kitchens can tailor-make a design to suit you, whether traditional or contemporary. They plan, create and install your choice and that includes any plumbing, re-wiring or decorating.

Planning your own contemporary kitchen

For those on a more modest budget, most DIY stores now offer a 3-D planning service. They won't come out to you, but if you take your measurements into the store, they input them into the computer and you can see what works in your kitchen plan. You might not be able to afford real granite or marble worktops but there are now so many stylish yet cheaper alternatives on offer: the room doesn't have to look as though you've cut corners. Just check that their cabinets are sturdy – remember the fitting counts here too – and that the hinges are good.

Kitchen appliances

You really don't have to spend a fortune to update a kitchen. Buy a trendy new kettle and toaster, paint the walls white, change the handles on the old units, replace the taps, lay a smart vinyl floor and install a couple of spotlights. You can do a lot for £300.

The second thing to do is to plan the layout. The all-important kitchen triangle is the cornerstone of the most conveniently designed kitchens. This works on the premise that the sink, fridge and cooker

Add some New Classic chic to your kitchen

Buying new appliances for the kitchen can be a minefield. The last thing you want to do is swap your hard-earned cash for a dust-gathering gimmick that takes up valuable space at the back of the cupboard. The solution to this age-old shopping dilemma comes in the form of the **New Classics Waring** range of kitchen essentials – a collection of appliances that mix superior performance with undisputed style.

If you want to be able to whiz up healthy smoothies or devilish cocktails from the comfort of your own home, plump for the Original Retro Blender by **Waring**. First manufactured in the 1930s, this blender is built to last but does not cut corners on style. Available in a choice of seven classic finishes, prices start at £159.

For maximum versatility, try the sleek SmartPower Blender (SSP £109) with its 5 powerful speed settings. The chic chrome base combines with a graduated heat resistant jug for practicality and designer flare. Add the new **Waring** Food Processor Attachment (SSP £39.95) if you want all the benefits if a compact food processor without having to splash out on a whole new appliance.

For multi-tasking, nothing tops the functional yet fashionable Mini-Prep Plus food processor (SSP £56). This dinky appliance features the new auto-reversing SmartPower blade, which spins anti-clockwise to chop or puree with the sharp edge, or clockwise to grind with the dull edge.

As everyone knows, cordials can never compete with the taste of fresh, unadulterated juice. The new contemporary Juice Extractor (SSP £109) is quick, efficient, and you can even put the removable parts in a dishwasher - ideal for today's healthy living, fast-paced lifestyle. For the serious juice fanatic, the commercial quality Juicerator (SSP £319) squeezes up to 95% of available juice from fruit and unpeeled vegetables for a maximum vitamin hit. Comes complete with filter papers, making cleaning a dream.

For further information on all of the above, plus details on the **NEW** Two To Go coffee filter machine, call **New Classics** direct on 01707 265465.

Classic lines finished in sleek silver, our new Satin collection is the ultimate in kitchen cool. And behind the looks lie some smart features... the kettle boasts a powerful 3kw concealed element, 360° easy fit power base and a sensible, wide angled spout, while the toaster can reheat, defrost, as well of course, make perfect toast...

start your day
in style

KENWOOD
MAKING GREAT FOOD SIMPLE

Dyson, DVD and DECO GLAZE.
Every now and then a product comes along
and completely revolutionises the industry.

DECO GLAZE Colour Coated glass is a sexy new alternative to stone, wood and stainless steel. It is a safe, permanent & efficient means of producing high quality decorative glass products. DECO GLAZE can be used for splashbacks, worktops and wall panelling etc.

The Colour Coating is applied by spray to the back of glass and is specially formulated to guarantee adhesion. The coating is resistant to heat, acid, alkali, humidity, permeability and ultra violet light – all verified by independent tests. DECO GLAZE offers a 10 year replacement Guarantee on the Colour Coat and a 90 day Replacement Installation Guarantee when installation is carried out by DECO GLAZE professionals using no visual fixings.

DECO GLAZE uses British quality Opticlear glass, this allows us to produce a wide variety of colours including beautiful metallic finishes. All our glass worktops are toughened for safety and strength, allowing the glass to withstand heat.

DECO GLAZE

If you would like more information or a proposal please contact us on:
tel: 020 8569 8585 fax: 020 8569 8586 email: info@decoglaze.co.uk or www.decoglaze.co.uk

BRITANNIA – IT'S ALL ABOUT CHOICE

The Range Cooker Company really do spoil you when it comes to choice. Their quality Britannia range cookers are available in 60cm, 90cm, 100cm, 120cm & 150cm width options and the company states they offer one of the widest selections of range cookers in the UK – over 160 model combinations of Britannia dual fuel and all electric cookers alone plus a comprehensive selection of chimney hoods and accessories.

Choose from traditional, modern and ultra modern styles to complement any kitchen furniture design.

Models with gas hotplates incorporating such features as triple ring burners – ideal for wok cookery, elongated burners for fish kettles, griddles and oval pans, rapid and semi-rapid burners too.

There are even models with lava stone barbeques and cast iron cooking/simmering zones. Britannia's latest development is a hotplate incorporating a gas fry top. This is a quality item manufactured in 8mm thick stainless steel and is ideal for cooking a variety of foods – meats, steaks, chicken, fish, numerous vegetables, onions, tomatoes, breakfast foods, eggs, omelettes, drop scones, welsh cakes, stir fries etc. It's ideal for Japanese style Tapanyaki cooking too. All the gas hotplates within the Britannia range are convertible to LPG (bottle gas) if so desired.

Alternatively you can opt for an all electric model which features an entire ceramic glass hotplate with up to six cooking zones. Some of the zones are dual type to give a choice of cooking area to suit various pan diameters. All zones are powered by the hi-tech, extremely reliable ribbon elements which give ultra quick response and one of the fastest boil times of any ceramic heaters in the world. The all electric range cookers are available in the choice of 90cm and 100cm width options.

The ovens on Britannia range cookers are electric multifunction which offers the cook the choice of nine functions – yet so simple to operate. Cooks can decide between true fan cooking, fan assisted cooking/grilling and conventional cooking/grilling. Defrost and slow cooking functions too. There's even a fast pre-heat system 'Quickstart' which brings the oven to 150° in 5 minutes.

Yet more choice –Britannia cookers are available in classic steel, classic midnight blue, classic emerald green, classic graphite, modern stainless steel and modern graphite. Britannia's ultra modern Dynasty range cookers are available exclusively in stainless steel.

Britannia – spoilt for choice!

BRITANNIA

RANGE COOKERS

CHOICE...

These are just a few of the 150 + models and
variations available from Britannia Range Cookers.
Unequalled legendary quality with sizes from
60 - 150cm to complement your lifestyle.
Send for the new comprehensive Brochure today.

Telephone 01253 47111
Fax: 01253 471136
Web: www.rangecooker.co.uk

Or visit our London Viewing
Showrooms, The Building Centre,
26 Store Street off Tottenham
Court Road.

Traditional Quality from: THE RANGE COOKER CO · PLC · Range House · Bristol Avenue · Blackpool FY2 0JF

should all be close together and easily accessible from one to the other. If your fridge-freezer is the tall style, keep it at the end of the worktop, not in the middle. And the route between the sink and the cooker is the busiest so keep it free of clutter. Think about the plan logically; try and keep all the plumbing – sink, dishwasher and washing machine – in the same area. Put the crockery cupboards near the dishwasher. Don't put the oven too close to the fridge and keep the kettle near the cups, spoons and coffee and tea.

Range cookers

After the kitchen units, the most expensive purchase in the kitchen is likely to be the cooker. Most modern kitchens incorporate a separate hob and oven. And perhaps because of the popularity of the Aga, range cookers are becoming more common. Standing alongside the Aga or Rayburn cooker, is now an increasing selection of other range cookers, most of them adapted for a modern kitchen. They're not as big or complicated to use and look very attractive. But care needs to be taken if you are having a range cooker installed. Many of them need a chimney or have to be fitted on an outside wall where they can have a flue. They do take up more room than a conventional cooker and can look out of place within a run of very contemporary units, but they are sought after and, unfortunately, sometimes their prices reflect that.

Staircases and landings

Unless there's a natural divider between the hall, the stairs and the landing, I suggest painting the three areas the same colour, preferably using a bright shade. This keeps a narrow space, and usually quite a dark one, more open and light. Tough flooring is a must and, if you skimp, anywhere else, don't do it here. Buy the most hardwearing carpet or stair runner you can afford. It's a false economy to do anything else, as you will be replacing a worn and dirty carpet every two years. If you can stand the noise, varnished floorboards look great and are cheap and hard-wearing. Be warned – check you can get any new beds and wardrobes up the stairs before you buy them.

Bedrooms

According to the people who collate those kind of useless facts and figures, we spend as much as a third of our lives in the bedroom. We might spend much of that time asleep, but that's precisely why we have to pay considerable attention to them.

How Many? After 'how much is it?' the second most asked question from a would-be buyer is 'how many bedrooms?' By adding a bedroom you will invariably add value, by removing one, the price will drop accordingly. That's the general rule of thumb, but there are exceptions. Two spacious and well-decorated rooms are a better bet than three tiny, cramped cells. And if one of the bedrooms is so small and out-of-proportion to the others, then turning it into an en suite bathroom may even up the price.

Beds and bedding

Because we spend so much of our lives in them, it's important to invest in the right kind of bed. This is a purchase that can't be rushed. Go to a large showroom and spend as long as it takes to find a comfortable and supportive mattress. Bed heads are a decorative feature and you can chop and change them for a couple of hundred pounds – or even make your own – but a decent mattress is a necessity and should last a decade. That's usually two house moves.

A bed is likely to be the largest piece of furniture in the room, there's no disguising it, so dress it up and flaunt it! Cheap bedding is one of the best bargains in the home improvement market. You can even buy quilts and duvet covers at supermarkets. Decide on how you want the room decorated and you will have no trouble finding bed linen to match. Or

SLEEP WELL, LIVE WELL!

We spend around a third of our lives asleep, and it's not time wasted! Good quality, regular sleep is essential to our continued physical and mental wellbeing. Just one night's disturbed sleep can leave us feeling irritable, unable to concentrate, generally rundown and less able to do even the most routine things. A recent Australian study shows that going without sleep can be as bad for driving as being over the legal alcohol limit.

So what is sleep?

Sleep is when the body gets busy doing essential maintenance work. During deep sleep, the body's blood cells, tissues and the immune system all benefit from 'in-house repairs'.

There are very important psychological benefits too. It's thought that dreaming helps the mind deal with the day's information. A brain 'in neutral' has the chance to sort things out, without the constant demands of running the daily consciousness getting in the way.

Sleep stoppers

Sleep therapists often recommend relaxation techniques and a little exercise during the day as basic aids to sleep. They'll also tell you to avoid drinking tea or coffee and eating large meals well before bedtime.

If you're a smoker, absorbing nicotine even hours before bed can make it harder to get to sleep. And while alcohol seems to help you relax, it actually upsets your sleeping patterns, so you don't get the quality of sleep your body needs.

Bedroom basics

Of course, dealing with all these factors won't help if you're sleeping environment isn't right!

Quiet and calm are bedroom essentials, plus a temperature that's not too hot or cold – about 16°C is thought to be ideal.

But the most important thing to consider is your bed, particularly in terms of the mattress and bedding you choose. The ideal mattress is one that's supportive without being hard; when choosing a new one make sure you lie on it for several minutes to ensure the mattress feels right. Most mattresses are well past their best at ten years old, and as sleep is so important to day-to-day wellbeing, it makes sense to choose carefully, and buy the best you can afford.

The making of a beautiful bed

Comfort in bed is everything, and as we spend about a third of our life there, it's good to make bed as refreshing and pleasant a place to be as possible. Obviously we should regularly wash sheets and pillowcases, but what about the duvet and the pillows themselves?

With Spundown duvets from The Fine Bedding Company you can wash even the king-size version without hassle, and keep your bed delightfully fresh as a result. That's because they've been designed to compress easily, to fit any domestic washing machine and are washable at 60°C, the temperature that kills dust mites.

Most pillows – even washable ones – tend to get lumpy, flat and uncomfortable over time. Contrastingly, Spundown washable pillows actually become plumper and more supportive with repeated washing and tumble drying. Their unique ball-cluster filling won't clump together to form lumps like the materials in other washable pillows and the Spundown pillow also washes at 60°C. So improving your existing bedroom or even moving into a new home is a great time to replace your duvet and pillows – start afresh and be able to keep it that way.

Sleeping with a Partner

Women's metabolic rates tend to be slower than men's and consequently women generate less personal heat. The problem is, when you share the same duvet one of you is likely to be too hot or too cold. In that case it's worth considering The Fine Bedding Company's Partner duvet, a one-piece duvet with a cooler half for the man and a warmer half for women.

Mild or occasional insomnia can often be solved by simple means, such as those covered here. But if you suffer from more serious sleeplessness, visit to your GP is the best course of action.

www.finebedding.co.uk

A duvet that bounces back...wash after wash!

the duvet that loves to be washed

Whatever you get up to, a Spundown duvet can take it.
Our technologically advanced fibre filling compresses easily, so even a
kingsize pops into a domestic washing machine. What's more the duvet
can be washed at 60°C, the safe and clean way to eliminate dust mites.
It's fresh thinking that means you can enjoy the feeling of a delightfully
clean duvet whenever you like.

**Call 0845 30 20 200 for your nearest stockist or visit House
of Fraser, Allders and good linen shops everywhere.**

THE **FINE BEDDING**
Company

FRESH THINKING

do it the other way round and use a stunning patchwork quilt or trendy, embroidered pillowcase as a starting point for your theme.

Bedroom furniture

As to the rest of the furniture, do you have freestanding pieces or do you want fitted wardrobes? The choice depends mainly on personal taste, but, obviously, built-in cupboards and drawers are more 'space-effective' in a smaller room and freestanding chests and armoires usually need a larger room to set them off.

Some furniture may have to do two jobs. If there's no space for a separate study, a dressing table may have to double as a desk, or think about those wardrobe-look-alikes which, when opened, show a computer with a pull-out keyboard shelf. And if you're short of storage, buy beds with drawers and build wardrobes to the ceiling to give space at the top. One eye-catching idea is to tear out the middle of a chimneybreast and fit it with extra shelves.

If there's only one bathroom, and the bedrooms have space, you might think about putting in a little vanity unit or sink and mirror. It cuts down on the queues for the bathroom each morning.

For a peaceful night's sleep, noise levels have to be low. This is where you might find double-glazing a necessity if your home is by a road or in the middle of a busy area. Also monitor noise from your neighbours. If only a slim partition wall divides your room from nextdoor's crying baby and those 3am feeds, think about losing a little space and fitting a secondary wall before you decorate.

Light is another factor. If the sun shines in too early, then curtain fabric and lining in a darker colour are going to help more than the currently fashionable muslin look. If you really need it, blackout material is easily bought, and many children's shops stock blinds and curtains already made up with it. Blinds always look nice and can be 'dressed' with ornamental curtains at the side to add interest. If you want to splash out and the room suits them, made-to-measure shutters look wonderful and are so flexible when it comes to privacy and light.

And So To Bed

We spend a third of our lives in our bedroom and yet ironically it is often the last to be decorated. With the demands from modern life growing, the bedroom is the ultimate private domain, a place to escape – a real retreat from the world.

The perfect bedroom is a multi-sensory experience; the room should look beautiful ... the bed should feel sublimely comfortable, bedlinens and fabrics should all demand to have a hand stroked across them ... it should even smell beautiful.

And So To Bed shops are dedicated to making bedrooms perfect. They sell beds which range from unashamed romance to witty eccentricity, together with sumptuous mattresses, crisp bedlinens and furniture which completes the look.

And So To Bed's exclusive designs include lovingly distressed copies of antiques and pieces with a more contemporary feel designed by the in-house team. There are beds made from wood, from brass and from forged and cast metal. What they share is an attention to detail and the robust, hand finished construction that takes the bed beyond a fashion statement and turns it into an heirloom.

Exclusive to **And So To Bed** is a collection of exquisite linens including duvet covers, pillowcases and sheets in natural linens, cottons and silks, often with lavish embroidery and drawn threadwork. Colours go from snowy whites through to vivid modern colourways. There are also bedspreads, pillows, duvets and sumptuous quilts, together with the ultimate in bed comforts … cashmere blankets and throws.

The heart of any good bed is its mattress and **And So To Bed** offers an excellent range of top quality pocket sprung mattresses – available with or without beds! To the untrained eye one mattress looks much like another, but beneath the surface their inner workings differentiate them and the support they provide. **And So To Bed** trained mattress consultants are on hand to offer and advice and guidance and when it comes to the quality of fillings and the different spring combinations and will suggest trying a variety of styles to see which mattress is suitable.

The bed may be centre stage, but it needs a supporting cast to show it off. **And So To Bed** make stylish bedside tables, armoires, chests and dressing tables – as well as smaller accessories including mirrors, stools and lamps. The range of looks includes French provincial and 'Gothic', an important design with ornate detailing.

And So To Bed has eighteen showrooms across England, Scotland and Northern Ireland.

The London flagship store is at 638 Kings Road, London SW6
Tel: 0808 144 4343 for brochures and branch details
www.andsotobed.co.uk

AND SO TO BED
—LONDON—

AN INSPIRATIONAL
COLLECTION OF EXCLUSIVE
DESIGNS, REPRESENTING
ONE OF THE FINEST AND
COMPREHENSIVE BEDSTEAD,
MATTRESS AND LINEN
COLLECTIONS AVAILABLE.

WWW.ANDSOTOBED.CO.UK
FREEPHONE 0808 144 4343

Bathrooms

Like kitchens, bathrooms are very important. A dirty, damp, depressing bathroom can put off even the most enthusiastic buyer or tenant. One of the reasons a would-be buyer may think again is the cost of fitting a new bathroom suite. Even the most dedicated DIY-er will probably have to get a plumber in here, and if there's any upgrading to be done in terms of electrics, damproofing or pumps for power showers, don't waste time trying to do it yourself. Get a couple of quotes and call in the experts.

Like Henry Ford said about his cars: 'Any colour as long as it's black.' Well, with bathrooms, it's got to be white. No avocado, no mushroom, no turquoise, at least not for the bath, sink and lavatory. White gives the impression of cleanliness and that's important in the smallest room in the house. It also appeals to more people, and one day you might want to sell.

Take a look at the layout of the room. If you're fitting a new suite it's cheaper and easier to keep the plumbing pipes where they are, but check that everything is in the most convenient place. If the loo is the first thing you see, try to move it.

A plain bathroom suite is cheapest and doesn't date as quickly as a decorated one. And go for simple chrome fittings. You may like gold taps, but with all the other accessories – loo-roll holder, towel rails and soap dish – supposed to match, it can become a bit too garish.

If there's space for a walk-in shower, do fit one. If not then put one over the bath. This is the 21st century and a shower is an absolute necessity. And not one which offers just a pathetic trickle of lukewarm water. Ask your plumber if you need a pump to boost the water pressure. Always have a mixer tap on the bath even if there's a shower too.

If you are pressed for space, shop around for suites designed on a smaller scale for tiny areas. Even corner baths can now be found in a smaller size, and there's a whole range of 'thin' lavatories and sinks. If there isn't enough room for a radiator fitted from the floor, put it on the wall and it doubles up as a towel rail. Exactly how small is the room? Is it worth having a spacious shower room rather than a cramped bathroom?

Small Bathroom? Small Problem!

Today most of us want more rooms in our homes. En-suite bathrooms, walk-in wardrobes and studies, are high on the 'hit-list'. Although these 'additional spaces' are being added, overall the sizes of properties is not getting any larger. As a result, rooms are small we need to make the most of the space available. The bathroom – 'the smallest room' in the house – is no exception to this.

Research has found that the average family bathroom is no larger than a king-sized bed. En-suites and even second family bathrooms are increasingly popular in, with this in mind, Britain's best known bathroom manufacturer, Ideal-Standard produced a bathroom suite that was both designed to fit neatly and purposely into small bathrooms and best of all make use of every inch of available space.

Ideal-Standard then carried out a survey in which one hundred of Ideal-Standard's customers supplied drawings and dimensions of their bathrooms, of which the six smallest and most awkward were recreated using full-scale models, in what became known as the 'Space Lab'. Prototype products designed by Royal Designer for Industry Robin Levien, were then installed, tested and altered accordingly within these model bathrooms until the perfect product was produced.

The result was the award winning Space range.

Space is not only designed to make the most of every available inch of space in the home. The sloping rooms and awkward corners of additional bathrooms are brought into use with products that help to fill 'dead' spaces.

When fitting the Space suite into a family bathroom, typical installation challenges such as the basin overhanging the bath are solved. In this instance with the Space narrow basin.

Short-projection basins prevent un-necessary intrusion into the rest of the bathroom and in return make the bathroom appear larger.

The Space offset shower bath, available in both left and right hand versions, is shorter and wider than the standard size bath and has an extra wide 'foot' end which becomes the showering space. Co-ordinated with the specially designed shower screen, a shower fitting over the Space bath eliminates the need for a separate shower cubical, once seen as an essential addition to a bathroom.

Space WC suites incorporate a number of innovative designs. Corner WCs fit neatly into un-used corners demonstrating Space's philosophy of making the most of every available space. All Space WCs come with the option of having the seat at a 45° angle. With the seat angled in this way, the WC suite can be fitted closer to the wall or to other sanitary ware. The Space WC can be fitted as close-coupled suite, corner close-coupled suite or as a back-to-wall suite.

The latest addition to Space is a range of fully fitted bathroom furniture. Space furniture neatly optimises living space and conceals plumbing, as well as saving space.

For the past four years, since its launch in 1998, the Space range has won many awards for its innovative design. Included amongst them are: the FX International Design Award for Best Residential Fitting; The Design Council Millennium Product status, a scheme recognising innovation, creativity and design; and the 1999 D&AD Silver Award for Most Outstanding Product for the Home, beating off strong competition, which included the iMac Apple Computer. This year Space added the Your Home/Daily Mail Ideal Home Show award for Best Bathroom Product.

For stockist information or to order a Space brochure call Ideal-Standard on:
0800 590311 or visit **www.ideal-standard.co.uk**

Ideal-Standard
The Bathroom Works
National Avenue
Kingston-Upon-Hull
HU5 4HS
Tel: 0800 590311
www.ideal-standard.co.uk

space

you've more in an **ideal** world

Ideal Standard

Ideal Standard Ltd The Bathroom Works Hull HU5 4HS
www.ideal-standard.co.uk e-mail: ideal.standard@aseur.com Tel: 0800 228476 Fax: 01482 445886

If there's another bath in the house, losing one and having a very trendy 'wet room' installed, won't cut the value. Ditto if you live in the kind of property, a flat perhaps, which is unlikely to be lived in by older people or children. But most estate agents will tell you that in an ordinary family home, they expect to see a bath – even if it is tiny.

There's also a debate raging about the number of loos a house should have. The typical newly built family home is given a downstairs lavatory, as well as an en suite bathroom and a family bathroom. That's three loos and seems plenty to me. If your property is an old one with just the traditional one bathroom, there's usually enough room to fit a second lavatory under the stairs. If you're considering a loft conversion, think about an extra bathroom or loo too. Don't add two bedrooms in the loft, putting more pressure on the one bathroom. Try two smaller rooms with a shower room, or one large master en suite.

Following through on the clean lines of a white bathroom suite, and particularly if there's little space, stick to tiles for decorating. Choose your colour and style and put them all the way up to the ceiling for height and space. Again, I'd keep the look simple and not too heavily patterned. If you have a nice large room, you could tile around the areas likely to get wet, then paint or wallpaper the rest, add a chair, a bookshelf and some pictures.

Storage is always at a premium in family bathrooms. Think about built in sink-units with cupboards and drawers underneath. Or a run of bathroom cabinets down one wall. If you've had to box in any pipes, carry on the run and use it as shelving. If there's a nook, fit shelves or a door to make a cupboard.

Mirrors will make a space look larger, and fit downlighters as well as the overhead light. Some bathroom cabinets come supplied with lights inside and outside.

This is one area of the house where I don't recommend carpet. I know it's nice to step out onto after bath or shower, but you have to work so hard to keep it from getting damp and then mouldy that I don't think it's worth it. Tiles are easy to keep clean and dry. They can be cold underfoot but if you fit underfloor central heating there's no problem. Vinyl

A Visionary Concept.

The minimal framing and clean contemporary lines of Aqata's new door-less enclosure is *'le Mirage'*.

The integrated tray and impressive curved screen creates a safe and water tight barrier with concealed fixings providing hidden strength and rigidity.

Also available with a unique curved sidescreen.

Open your imagination,
for a free brochure please call 01455 896500.

www.aqata.co.uk   email: sales@aqata.co.uk

SHOWER ENCLOSURES
for a lifetime of luxury

flooring is super. It's hard-wearing, easily dried and there's a huge choice of styles and colours. If you prefer bare floorboards, they're going to need an extra couple of coats of yacht varnish to make them waterproof.

The roof

You should have had a structural survey done when you bought the property and that would have given you a general description of the construction, the materials used and the condition of the timberwork, cladding, tiles, gutters and any insulation. You wouldn't have bought the property if there had been any major problems but, remember, prevention is better than cure and now you're the owner, any expense in the future will come out of your pocket. So do check regularly for any signs of trouble. Check to see the gutters aren't blocked by leaves or dirt – usually the cause of damp soaking through the walls. Mesh guards will prevent leaves being washed down pipes. Look out for any loose or missing tiles, or if the chimney needs to be repointed and that the TV aerial is securely attached.

Outside

The garden

The garden should be an extension of your living space, and no matter how small it is, any outside space is a value-added bonus when it comes to selling. You don't have to be Alan Titchmarsh to make any plot, whatever its size, a pretty and peaceful place to enjoy a glass of wine in the sunshine. Buy a lawnmower – they're as cheap as £30 – and a decent outdoor, hard brush for the paths.

After a weeding session, cover the ground with weed suppressing material and top that with bark chippings or gravel – no more weeds and a tidy bed. You may not be a natural gardener, but it doesn't take long to maintain a garden to a standard you don't mind sitting in. It has to be

LAWNFLITE – A COMPREHENSIVE RANGE OF GARDEN EQUIPMENT

Lawnflite has been a much loved brand of powered gardening equipment for many years, offering a comprehensive range for everyone's gardening needs.

With a line up of ride-on tractors ranging from the Lawnflite 404 multi-purpose utility rider offering a 24"/610mm cut with a 6.5hp Briggs & Stratton engine up to the Lawnflite 908 with a 41"/1040mm cut and an 18hp Briggs & Stratton V Twin Intek engine, Lawnflite caters for the smaller garden right up to a garden of 4 acres. With the exception of the Lawnflite 503 which has an integral collection system, all Lawnflite Tractors have the 'direct collect'(r) system which has been designed to cope with the lush, wet grass plus the normal damp conditions usually found throughout the UK. There are no expensive moving parts such as brushes, bearings, belts and pulleys to regularly maintain or replace. Wet cuttings are thrown direct from the blades, without touching the ground, straight through a large opening into the rear of the tractor, high into the bag where the grass circulates and is evenly distributed until the bag is full. When the bag is full, cuttings will drop to the ground and will not block the system. Some of the models offer audible warnings or the deck cuts out.

The new 500 series also offers the *FAST-ATTACH* system that allows attachments to be fitted in minutes without the need for tools. There is an extensive range of towed accessories such as trailers, sweepers, spreaders, sprayers, aerators, dethatchers, rollers and reel mowers which will fit all our 'direct collect'(r) tractors (with the exception of the 404), as all are fitted with a tow bar as standard.

All Lawnflite tractors come with a FREE optional second year warranty provided the tractor has been serviced by an appointed dealer within the first twelve months of purchase.

For those without the need for a ride-on tractor, Lawnflite offers a comprehensive range of petrol rotary mowers including the 478SPS fitted with the revolutionary Self Start system which uses the inertia of the engine when it stops to effectively tension springs inside the starter assembly – all it requires is a touch of a button for the engine to come to life and no battery is required. For those who like a beautifully striped lawn, the Lawnflite range of rotary mowers also includes rear roller models.

Other products in the Lawnflite range include domestic and professional brushcutters with either 2 or 4 stroke Robin or Kawasaki engines, all with electronic ignition, diaphragm carburettors, an anti-vibration system and feature a Sure-Tap head, allowing new nylon lines to be fed out simply by tapping the central button on the ground.

A superb range of petrol and electric hedgecutters are available, including the LR25PP Long Pole Pruner which offers an extra 6ft reach, has a powerful 25cc Robin engine and is ideal for pruning difficult to reach branches.

When autumn leaves and branches start to fall, Lawnflite cleans up your garden with a range of petrol and electric Chippers, Shredders, Vacs and Blower Vacs and, for those long cold winter evenings, Lawnflite has a range of electric log splitters.

To keep the grass in tip top shape Lawnflite has a range of Verticutters, Scarifiers and Lawn Edgers. For those who enjoy growing their own vegetables there are also Tillers available which will break up virgin ground to leave a fine tilth.

E P Barrus Ltd are also the UK Distributors of the MTD Yardman range of rotary mowers and ride-on tractors plus the MTD Cub Cadet range of tractors with a cutting width of up to 54"/1370mm and a 23hp engine for the really large garden.

Whatever your gardening needs – Lawnflite can help.

For further information on any Lawnflite products please contact
Angie Jamieson
E P Barrus Ltd
Launton Road
Oxon OX26 4UR
Tel. 01869 363606
E-mail: angie.jamieson@barrus.co.uk
www.barrus.co.uk

said though, that a garden left to run wild and overgrown, or a patio or terrace neglected and weed-covered, is going to detract from the appeal of your property.

Gates and fences

Fit a decent garden gate, either in wood if you like the picket fence look, or iron. Remember that decent gates – front and back – are also security features. Repair fences, paint an old shed, and plant up a few pots with bright flowers.

Other security features

Most new windows and doors have to conform to regulations that aim to improve household security and therefore have proper locks. If you've replaced windows and doors and already have new double glazing, then, alongside a burglar alarm and decent outside lighting, that's probably as much as you will want. If you are not replacing windows and doors, fitting tough locks and latches is a necessity. It is probably a condition of your insurance policy. For those who want a higher level of security, a security expert or a visit from the police, will point you in the right direction. Proximity alarms, floodlighting and sensors are all easily available. If you work from home and have reason to keep large sums of money there, think about having a hidden safe set into the floor or a 'secret' cupboard built for valuables.

Gates may be the final touch to your property but they are also the first impression any visitor will have. Whether you have a wide sweeping ornate iron work-of-art at the front of your drive, or a small wooden gate at the end of your back garden, a gate can really enhance the look of your property and provide privacy and distinct territorial boundaries.

Cannock Gates, based in Staffordshire are well known as one of the finest manufacturers and mail order suppliers of high quality wrought iron and timber gates. Established twenty years ago, our gates adorn literally thousands of properties the length and breadth of mainland UK.

Drive gates, field gates, front gates and side gates – with over 600 styles and size combinations available, we offer something for every taste and situation. It's important to choose a gate that's in keeping with the style of your house, then keep it well maintained and looking good. Our wooden gates are supplied with a cedar base coat and once installed, should be treated with a high quality wood preservative. Our wrought iron gates are supplied with a primed black finish and should be treated with high-quality metal finish paint.

For extra security, luxury and convenience, many of our gates can be made suitable for automation. We offer above and below ground automation kits, with a range of optional extras such as intercom sets and digital keypads.

We provide a comprehensive range of posts, fittings and accessories and most importantly, we have an advisory service to help you if you're not sure of exactly what you need, or how to measure up.

To request a copy of our latest catalogue, call **08707 54 75 75**.

If you have access to the Internet, log on to www.cannockgates.co.uk to see our full range of gates and garden products. You can also request a catalogue or buy on line. Or why not visit our Factory Shop in Cannock?

Micromark Makes Securing Your Home Simple

Home security is a sensible investment that will not only help you feel more secure in your own home but add to its market value when you decide to sell.

Research commissioned by Micromark* found 8 out of 10 burglars were put off by home CCTV, alarms and security lighting when considering a break-in.

The research revealed that when given a choice between a property with an open window and home CCTV or a house without CCTV and all windows locked, 8 in 10 said they would opt to burgle the house without CCTV, despite the fact that it would be more difficult to break into.

When surveying a property for points of entry, 6 in 10 of those questioned cited 'back doors' and about half 'windows above flat roofs' as the easiest ways to break into a home. These are some of the first areas to consider when installing CCTV cameras.

Despite the findings of this research, few households have domestic CCTV systems installed. Common misconceptions about domestic CCTV are that it is expensive, difficult to install and unsightly. However, Micromark CCTV systems start from as little as £29.99 and alarms from only £9.99 – a small price to pay for peace of mind.

Considering this relatively low outlay, security products actually have a high perceived value, adding market value to your property. New home buyers can move straight in, with no installation to carry out but know that they are secure.

And you don't need to be a DIY expert. Micromark CCTV systems are easy to install. With no wiring required, the whole process takes less than 30 minutes!

Simply plug the systems straight into your existing TV to give high quality images and sound at the touch of a button.

Micromark CCTV systems, alarms and security lights all come with fully illustrated step-by-step instructions and the support of a technical helpline.

Micromark's home security product range includes: Automatic Video Starting CCTV Systems (MM23142/MM23214, RRP. £79.99-£99.99) come complete with a built-in PIR (Passive Infra Red) sensor that detects movement, and can be set to  automatically change your TV channel to show the CCTV picture whenever someone approaches. There's also an option to sound a buzzer if you do not wish to interrupt your TV viewing. The CCTV system will then start your video; recording the movement detected. Some systems will also stamp the time and date onto the recording and have a two-way intercom (MM23214 only).

The Wirefree Burglar Alarm System (MM23216, RRP. £179.95) provides a simple and effective way to secure your home. There is absolutely no wiring to be done, so it's ideal for DIY installation. The kit includes: a siren/control box; two wirefree PIR (passive infra red) sensors which detect movement; a wirefree door/window contact and a remote key-fob to operate the system. It comes with a unique detachable key-pad that can be used from anywhere in the home. The alarm also incorporates a panic button that activates the siren when held down for 5 seconds. You can add to this alarm system by buying additional sensors to suit your needs.

The Evolution® Energy Efficient Security Floodlight (MM4900, RRP. £29.99) is the first floodlight to be endorsed by the Energy Saving Trust. It is designed to offer effective yet environmentally friendly security lighting. Evolution® consumes 70% less energy than standard 500W floodlights, thereby reducing your energy bill by approximately £20 per year (compared to a standard 500W floodlight). And as an added bonus, the Evolution® also has a built in energy saving "all night" low-level light option, offering you comfort and security at an affordable price.

Micromark security products are available from Argos, B&Q, Focus, Homebase and leading independent retailers.

For more information, call Micromark on 020 8829 6354, email info@micromark.co.uk or visit www.micromark.co.uk

*NOP surveyed 25 people who have been convicted of burglary in the past 18 months, dated 29 May – 5 June 2002

It doesn't have to be a fortress to be secure

Simple affordable security from Micromark

Security Lighting

from £8.99*

CCTV Systems

from £29.99*

Alarm Systems

from £24.99*

Whether your home is a studio flat or a mansion, Micromark have an easy to install security product for you. Security products have a very high perceived value, so for a little outlay you can not only make your home secure but also increase its market value.

With a wide range of DIY products that includes Security Lanterns and Floodlights, the latest in home CCTV Systems and a complete range of Intruder Alarms, Micromark has the product to fit your home and your pocket.

Micromark products are available from Argos, B&Q, Focus, Homebase and leading Independent Retailers.

For further details on the full range of Micromark Security products and more stockists call 020 8829 6354 quoting DEBG0203

micromark
QUALITY THAT'S GUARANTEED

*Prices do not necessarily relate to products shown.

Surprise!

You never know what you might find when you leave your home empty for a day, a weekend, a fortnight... installing an ADT security system can help ensure that you don't have any unwanted surprises when you return. **To find out how ADT can help you protect your home from intruders and fire...**

Call now on 0800 010 999

(quoting ref. DE01)

HOW SAFE & SECURE IS YOUR HOME?

Let's face it, when it comes to splashing out on your home, security is rarely top of anyone's shopping list. It just isn't sexy, is it? Not like a new state-of-the-art stereo system, a widescreen TV or a leather sofa. Which is too bad, especially when you return from holiday to find a burglar has helped themselves to your expensive goodies or, worse still, they've been reduced to ashes.

It's a sad fact that most of us only install a burglar or fire alarm after a break-in or near miss with a saucepan on the stove. The statistics say it all – 5.6% of UK homes are burgled every year, 40% of which happen while someone is in. As for fires, three out of four occur at home, with one breaking out roughly every eight minutes.

Yet it's not all doom and gloom, as ADT Fire and Security, the UK's leading fire and security company, outlines.

"Security is a subject that people tend not to think about until something goes wrong, but we are working hard to change that attitude," says ADT's Home Security Marketing Manager, Christina Poulsen. "People are starting to realise that it is worth spending a little time and money safeguarding their home, to prevent the heartache that a burglary or fire can cause."

In the past, ordinary 'bell' burglar alarms proved popular with householders simply because they were cheap and readily available. However, due to the rising number of false alarms, many police forces have adopted a policy of refusing to attend ringing alarms.

However, with an ADT monitored alarm, you'll be able to go about your daily business with peace of mind. Because in the event of it being activated, the ADT Alarm Receiving Centre knows about it instantly, and will call your home within seconds. If necessary, the centre will summons help from the emergency services immediately.

Monitored alarms can go one step further by protecting you against more than just the threat of burglars. Panic buttons can be added to a system, enabling you to get help should you be attacked at home. Other systems also allow you to send a secret alarm signal should an intruder force you to switch off the main alarm against your will.

Traditional smoke alarms are without doubt effective but, like the old bell alarms, have their faults. Be honest now – how often do you check the batteries in yours?

ADT's revolutionary CO Fire Detector is regarded as being in a league of its own, as it protects properties even when the alarm isn't switched on. The detector responds to carbon monoxide, the toxic gas which is produced in smouldering fires, and therefore reacts faster than the average smoke alarm.

Otherwise known as 'the silent killer', carbon monoxide kills around 50 people each year in the UK, injuring many hundreds more, its drowsy effects often being mistaken for a common cold or flu.

It was a CO Fire Detector that saved Holkham Hall – the Norfolk home of the Earl and Duchess of Leicester and a favourite with Hollywood film producers – from serious damage. Two months after it was fitted by ADT, a detector picked up traces of carbon monoxide inside one of the building's many rooms, enabling staff to move in and extinguish a small fire before it started spreading.

"What happened at Holkham Hall shows that no matter how large or small your home is, it really does pay to protect it properly," adds Christina. "Apart from securing your property, it could even save your life."

The stress of moving house is ranked higher than divorce! Just to add to this, moving leaves both your old and new premises vulnerable to the opportunist thief. House doors are often left open for short periods (while you are storing your boxes in the removal van or car) and if he were seen walking down your path with a box, observers would assume he was a bona fide removal man.

Do you know if you have been handed all the keys to your new home? Do you know everyone who had prior access to your keys? If its a new property, all the tradesman would have required access, were all the keys handed back? Do you know exactly how many keys have been cut for your locks before you took charge of them?So changing your locks as soon as possible following a move would be a lesser stress than dealing with a break-in (or a walk in and out).

12
Buying abroad

Points to consider

First of all you need to decide what you want out of a property overseas. Is it mainly for holidays, for a retirement home, for rental income or capital appreciation?

Five years ago two-thirds of people looking for property abroad were buying for retirement. Now at least a quarter are buying for investment and, although investment buyers are generally in their 40s and 50s with some spare money to hand, there is an increasing number of younger people looking for alternatives to paying into a pension.

Buying property abroad is becoming more attractive as the buy-to-let market in the UK looks increasingly vulnerable, and as the proliferation of cheap flights in and out of local airports gives a wider choice of area to buy in.

Most Britons want to buy in Spain – other popular destinations include France, Florida, Portugal and even as far afield as South Africa.

When deciding where to buy, personal preference will be influential, particularly if the property is to be used as a holiday home for some of the year. But experts advise buyers to do their research first.

Visit the area, investigate the prices of local properties yourself and find out what other people are doing. The location will determine for how many weeks of the year the property is likely to be let. In Tenerife, with warm year-round weather, you can expect your house or apartment to be let for 45 weeks annually. In the mainland tourist areas – usually close to a big city – of France or Spain, 25 weeks is more likely, while in more out-of-the-way rural areas only around 12 weeks through the summer is achievable.

The property should be near an airport or other excellent transport links, be nearby some local attractions, look good in a photo and be cared for between lets. Do think about your market – families want gardens and pools for children to play in, not wrought-iron balconies with stunning views over steep drops.

Many agents will organise a research trip to the area for prospective buyers. British Homes Abroad, for example, which markets property in Florida, will arrange an apartment for buyers to stay in while looking and will refund the cost of the stay if a purchase is made through them.

In general, investors can expect annual rental income of about 7.5 per cent of the value of the property, after deducting all expenses and including the costs of a managing agent. These generally charge between 15 per cent and 20 per cent of rent. For those who decide not to employ an agent, the time and expense of finding tenants, paying bills, cleaning, marketing and maintenance must be considered.

Buyers have two options when raising money to finance the purchase of a property abroad. The easiest is to borrow against a UK property, not necessarily in sterling, although this requires adequate equity available to finance the overseas purchase.

The second option is to borrow abroad against the property, which avoids currency risk. But there are generally fewer deals available than in the UK and you must feel confident about negotiating in another country. British Mortgages Abroad is a company that offers mortgages for buying property abroad through First National and Abbey National.

The maximum loan to value is between 75 per cent and 85 per cent and mortgages are not offered on the strength of anticipated rental income.

Mortgage broker Charcol advises that, because a deposit will be required and the costs associated with buying will be between 10 and 15 per cent, buyers will need a cash sum of between 30 and 35 per cent of the purchase price. Overseas mortgage specialists, such as Conti Financial Services, can give detailed advice on specific markets.

As well as financial advice, buyers will need legal guidance, preferably from a lawyer with a knowledge of UK law as well as the law of the country where the property is to be bought. A buyer also needs to be on top of the tax implications of owning property abroad before making an investment decision.

Rental profit on property abroad will be taxed in the UK, even if the money is kept overseas or reinvested in the property. Certain expenditure is deductible from rent, particularly upkeep of the property, but not capital expenses. Foreign tax payable on the rental profits can be credited against UK tax.

Euro mortgages

Taking out a mortgage in another country can mean access to cheaper borrowing rates. But the levels differ widely across the Continent, and some markets are less competitive than the UK.

UK-based borrowers will also have to remember that they are taking on additional currency risk with a euro-denominated loan. The stability of the euro is constantly called into question and if the value of the euro rises against sterling, borrowing costs will increase.

The arrangements for conveyancing and legal requirements associated with buying a house abroad can vary from country to country. But there is a growing number of specialist mortgage brokers and advisers who can hold homebuyers' hands through the process.

Conti Financial Services, based in Hove, East Sussex, produces a series of fact sheets to help prospective customers. Some of this information can also be found on its website at www.conti-financial.com.

France

Variable rate mortgages are available at 3.7 per cent with higher fixed rates. A repayment mortgage generally requires a 15 per cent deposit, with a 20 per cent down-payment needed for an interest-only loan.

All mortgages need to be accompanied by a life assurance policy, and with some lenders these come free.

A survey or valuation is not compulsory and many lenders do not conduct them, so borrowers may wish to organise their own.

All borrowers in France will need a French bank account and will need to show the lender proof of income. This involves at least three months' payslips or three years of audited accounts for the self-employed.

French lenders do not take into account the value of any rental income when calculating the affordability of the mortgage. They also require that all your existing liabilities, including any other mortgage or rent payments, personal and bank loans, credit cards and divorce mainte-nance payments – together with your proposed French mortgage – must not exceed 40 per cent of your net monthly income.

Spain

Variable rates are currently available from around 3.98 per cent, but early redemption penalties apply in many cases. Homebuyers have to pay a minimum deposit of 20 per cent.

Borrowers need to show proof of income and Spanish lenders do not take into account rent on the property in deciding whether you can afford the mortgage. The affordability of the loan is based on existing liabilities, together with the requirement that your proposed Spanish mortgage should not exceed 35 per cent of your net monthly income.

Borrowers are warned that they must obtain title to the property – the *nota simple* – often before a lender can carry out a valuation. Buyers of new property must have it registered in their name and not that of the builder before the loan can be secured. If your house is under construc-tion, Spanish banks will provide 'stage' financing in instalments, but only if it is registered in your name.

Fixed loans are available at 3.75 per cent for the first year with variable rates at 5.75 per cent. A deposit of 30 per cent is required and repayment mortgages only are offered.

Italy

Variable rates are on offer from 4.3 per cent with a minimum 20 per cent deposit. Repayment mortgages only are available and some discounted rates are available.

Borrowers need an Italian bank account and a tax code, which a lawyer will arrange. British homebuyers need to be aware that the Italian system is bureaucratic and can lead to delays in getting financing in place.

Portugal

Variable rates are at about 4 per cent, with a minimum deposit of 20 per cent. Some lenders are prepared to take into account rental income as well as salary and pension when calculating the level of loan on offer. A life policy is required when taking out a mortgage.

Eastern Europe

Some mortgage brokers are now turning to the EU's candidate countries as an investment opportunity for UK buyers. Countries such as Poland and the Czech Republic will join the EU in 2004 and some will place restrictions on purchases by overseas buyers. But some companies are finding ways round this – such as setting up a limited company in the country to buy the property.

Keeping healthy

No matter where in the world you and your family are moving to, it is essential to ensure you will have access to quality health care. International health cover gives you total peace of mind, as you will only ever be a phone call away from medical attention and advice.

In choosing an international health insurer, here are the main considerations to bear in mind:

- Make sure you choose an insurer that will provide worldwide cover, giving you help wherever and whenever you need it.
- It is best to select a scheme that covers:
  - immediate emergency care
  - referral to a specialist or hospital if necessary
  - therapist treatment
  - dental treatment
  - hospital treatment and in-patient care.
- Ensure you have 24-hour access to help and advice. A good insurer will have a multi-lingual helpline open every hour of every day of the year – to provide expert advice and support.
- Choose an insurer that has direct settlement arrangements with hospitals and clinics to save you time, money and inconvenience.
- Ensure you will be able to keep an eye on your scheme details and track individual claims online.
- Routine illness is the most common reason for making a claim, so it is important that you are protected against such eventualities. While many routine illnesses are considered fairly minor at home, they may be cause for concern if they occur overseas.

BUPA International is the world's largest expatriate health insurer, with over 30 years' experience of caring for the needs of expatriates. BUPA International is part of the BUPA Group, which looks after the health care needs of over eight million customers of 115 nationalities in 190 countries worldwide.

The BUPA International Lifeline schemes offer choice and flexibility. There are up to three levels of cover to choose from, each one appropriate for different circumstances.

Contact BUPA International on www.bupa-intl.com or call + 44 (0) 1273 208 181.

Health around the world

Travelling abroad means coming into contact with different kinds of health risks. Every country has its own health issues, endemic diseases and unique problems, but there is no need to worry as long as you are prepared. Detailed country-by-country health information and advice can be found online at the BUPA International site www.bupa-intl.com

Vaccinations

For extended trips or moves abroad, vaccinations are usually required. You and your family may have to take a medical examination and provide proof of immunisations before being granted entry into countries such as Australia, Canada and the USA.

The British Department of Health provides detailed lists of the inoculations needed for each country at www.doh.gov.uk/traveladvice. It is a good idea for you to seek personal advice from your family doctor too.

Prescription drugs

When taking drugs abroad, it is important to find out if there are any restrictions. Either ask the relevant embassy or call the Home Office Drugs Branch on +44 (0) 207 273 3806. Medicines that are widely available in the UK will not always be available abroad. It is important that you inform doctors, opticians, dentists and any other specialists of your move and organise any necessary repeat prescriptions. The website www.prescriptions.ltd.uk ensures that British nationals who are living abroad can organise a long-term supply of any medication you may need. It is wise for anyone with serious allergies or reactions to certain drugs to wear a medical bracelet to identify the specific problems.

Health checks

Before leaving home, every member of your family should have a thorough check-up to detect any potential health problems. This should be carried out at least two months in advance to permit any necessary treatment before departure.

Useful contacts:
www.bupa-intl.com
www.fco.gov.uk
www.cdc.gov
www.prescriptions.ltd.uk
www.netdoctor.co.uk

the world health service

wellbeing

From the moment you are born, your
wellbeing is in the hands of other people.
As you get older, your health continues to
be vital to your everyday life. Over five million
individuals in 190 countries rely on BUPA to look
after their health care needs, wherever they may be.

BUPA International - trust us to care.

THE QUEEN'S AWARD FOR
EXPORT ACHIEVEMENT

www.bupa-intl.com
+44 (0) 1273 208181

BUPA
International

13
Buying a home in Scotland

A different legal system

For anyone buying property in Scotland for the first time it is important to be aware of the correct way to go about it. This is particularly the case for anyone moving from England, as there are fundamental differences between the Scottish system and that operating 'South of the Border'.

Although the basics are the same, it is the timing of when the contract becomes legally binding that has led to two different approaches. It is important to understand that there is no second step in the Scottish procedure and that the contract can become legally binding at a relatively early stage, unlike in England where contracts are often exchanged towards the end of the process. In Scotland, they prefer not to wait until the removal men are at the door before exchanging contracts.

The contract takes the form of a series of letters known as missives, which are signed by the parties' solicitors. Once the offer has been accepted on all points, you have entered into a legally binding contract and neither party can withdraw without potentially being held liable for the consequent losses of the other party.

Accordingly, you should be careful and only put in an offer in Scottish legal form through your solicitor. If you offer in writing yourself and this is accepted you could end up being committed to buying a 'pig in a poke' – a well known Scots non-legal term!

The different legal systems have to be considered particularly carefully if you have a house to sell in England and you are relying on that sale to fund the purchase of a house in Scotland. You will require separate solicitors, and it is important that your English solicitor is aware of the need to progress the sale procedures as swiftly as possible.

Scottish solicitors

It may be tempting to think, 'surely I don't need another solicitor – it's just a case of filling in a form'. Certainly with Land Registration, the conveyancing part of the process is more straightforward but most properties in the Borders are still not registered. Even where the property has been registered, there are still aspects of the transaction that require a careful eye. Solicitors are used to dealing with buying properties. The length of a standard Scottish offer is built on the experience of problems that, to a lay person, would not be obvious. If you are borrowing from a bank or a building society, they will certainly require the security work to be done by a solicitor – so why take on any unnecessary worry?

You might think that, now we are all in the single market place in Europe, your solicitor in England should be able to deal with the purchase – but he can't. Scotland has its own separate and distinct legal system. The legal environment is different and you will require a Scottish solicitor to look after your interests. Although some agents do sell houses on either side of the border, the estate agency part of the selling process should not be confused with conveyancing. You will still need a Scottish solicitor.

The costs

As property prices have risen the Government has taken a bigger slice of the cake in terms of indirect taxes. Stamp duty is currently 1 per cent of purchases between £60,000 and £250,000, 3 per cent on properties between £250,000 and £500,000 and 4 per cent above that. This is payable on the whole of the price, so a purchase at £450,000 would involve a stamp duty bill of £13,500. On top of that there is the cost of registering the title, which, again, is charged on a sliding scale increasing with the value of the property.

If you ask a solicitor for a comprehensive breakdown, you might be pleasantly surprised at how the fee element compares. At the end of the day you will need a bottom-line figure for budgeting purposes. Any solicitor should be prepared to give you an indication of the likely costs at the outset of the transaction.

The asking price

In Scotland properties are usually marketed on an 'offers over' basis which is just an indication of the price that the seller is being advised to look for and does not mean that a lower offer would be refused. It will depend on the competition and various other factors. For example, if the property has been on the market for a while and there are no competing purchasers, it might be worthwhile offering less than the asking price and making your offer subject to a satisfactory survey.

An offer 'subject to survey' is less attractive to the seller as it puts the buyer in control, so if your offer were acceptable in principle, a seller would generally respond by setting a time limit for the survey to be done. This might be appropriate where you have a limited budget or there are particular circumstances but as a rule it is advisable to get a survey, or at least a valuation, first. An offer 'subject to survey' is unlikely to be accepted at a closing date unless it is considerably higher than the other offers.

Ready cash?

Do you need to have the cash available on the day you offer? Not strictly – you will only need the funds for the purchase at the settlement date – ie the date specified in your offer, which can be weeks but is more usually months ahead. This is when you will pay the price in exchange for getting entry to the property.

If you have a house to sell, particularly if the house is in England where a different system applies, you must be confident that the funds will be available or be prepared to take on bridging finance. If there is substantial equity in your home, some banks will still agree open-ended bridging and, with interest rates as low as they are at present, it might be worth taking a 'minimal risk' to secure the property of your dreams.

However, you should be careful and get the bank to put any bridging facility in writing.

Noting interest

If you don't want to miss out on a chance to offer, you should ask the selling agents to note your interest. In that way, if another party offers, you may be given an opportunity to submit a competing formal offer, in which case a closing date may be fixed. However, the selling agents are not bound to do so and if an acceptable offer comes in, the property might be sold without it going to a closing date.

Closing date

If a closing date has been set and you have noted your interest, you will be invited to submit your offer by a specific date and time. This system has its critics, as you are in a blind bidding situation, but it generally means that the seller achieves the best price and, where there are a number of interested parties, it gives each an opportunity to submit an offer. The downside is that you will incur costs, particularly for a survey, which will be no further use to you if your offer is unsuccessful.

If a closing date for offers is fixed, you will need to have done all your homework before you are ready to offer. It is advisable to have a survey carried out, and your funding arrangements should be in place. Your solicitor can instruct a surveyor (and obtain quotes from specialist contractors should treatment for woodworm, damp, dry/wet rot etc, be indicated) and help you find a mortgage, either directly or through a broker.

Concluding missives

If your offer is successful, your solicitor and the seller's solicitor will then negotiate the 'missives', which are the formal letters passing between them dealing with the finer points of the contract that will finally be concluded. Once 'missives have been concluded' (roughly equivalent to the exchange of contracts in England), you are contractually bound to buy the property at the agreed date of entry and the seller is contractually bound to sell. The date of entry may be some weeks, or even months ahead, and it is at that point that the full purchase price is payable.

On occasions the contract provides for a deposit payable at an earlier stage but usually only in the case of a new house, where the builders tend to dictate the terms. If a deposit is required, this should be clear from the sales particulars.

From that point, your solicitor will examine the title deeds provided by the seller's solicitor and prepare the 'disposition' (the document that will transfer the ownership of the property to you), liaise with your lender, prepare the loan documents, check all the necessary searches and ensure that the seller's title matches the title plan. Your solicitor will also report to you on any title conditions that could affect the property and restrict its use, and the appropriate clause to protect your position will have been included in your offer.

These are the main features that you should look out for when buying property in Scotland. It is not as daunting as it may seem and by discussing your plans with your solicitor at an early stage you will ease the process and avoid potential pitfalls.

Buyer beware

Below are some frequently-asked questions about the Scottish system.

Q. How do I make an offer?
A. A formal offer in Scotland is submitted in writing by your solicitor. You give him instructions and he signs the offer on your behalf. You sign nothing at all except, perhaps, loan papers.

Q. Can I make an offer before I have sold my house?
A. It is possible but probably not advisable. In Scotland a contract is formed within a relatively short time. If your offer is accepted, you may

find yourself in a position of having to pay the price on a particular day without having sold your own house. This is particularly disconcerting if you are used to the English system where you can pull out of a deal at the last minute. If this is likely to be difficult for you, you should not make an offer until you are certain of your own sale. It would be equally unwise to enter into an arrangement for bridging finance unless you were 100 per cent certain of your sale.

Q. Should I wait until I have had a survey carried out before submitting my offer?
A. There is no easy answer to this one. Normally a survey is carried out before the offer is submitted but if a closing date has been set (a deadline for offers to be received), then you may not have time. Your solicitor can often find out informally if the price you want to offer would be acceptable. This would be the best course of action if you want to offer less than the asking price.

Q. Is there freehold and leasehold in Scotland?
A. The system of landholding in Scotland is feudal in origin and, as owner, you will have rights, which can be passed on in perpetuity – similar to freehold. Leasehold is fairly rare for domestic properties in Scotland.

Q. What are missives?
A. When a Solicitor submits an offer for you he does so in letter form. The acceptance is also a letter. These letters form the missives. Sometimes an offer is accepted subject to certain conditions that the seller wants in the contract. This is called a 'qualified acceptance'. Once all matters are agreed, the 'bargain is concluded' and a contract is formed.

Q. Can foreigners buy Scottish property?
A. There is nothing to stop a foreigner buying Scottish property. There is no residence requirement and the property taxes are the same. Many foreigners own property from the smallest crofthouse to the largest of

hunting estates. Similarly, there is no reason why a foreigner cannot obtain a loan here, secured over the property, to fund part of the purchase.

Q. What is a croft?
A. Land that is registered croft land is available for anyone to purchase but an administrative body – called the Crofters Commission – regulates the occupation of crofts and may, if the land is not being properly utilised, impose a tenant upon the owner. That tenant would have rights to buy the land (but not the house if you were occupying one on the croft), usually for a very small sum.

The Crofting Acts were social engineering designed to ensure that there was land available for small-scale agricultural enterprise and to ensure that rural areas remained populated.

Buying land that is registered croft land, if it is not to be used for traditional activities such as keeping of cattle and sheep or growing crops, could result in dispossession of the land. Anyone buying and carrying out the traditional type activities should not have a problem.

If all you want to do is buy a house that has nothing beyond a garden, and it is described as a croft, there really is nothing to worry about.

Be sure to select a solicitor from the North of Scotland if you are buying a croft or crofthouse, as they tend to have more experience in this subject.

Q. What about taxes?
A. There are taxes on profits made on the sale of any property (land or buildings) that is not your main residence (Capital Gains Tax).

There is also a tax relating to residential property as opposed to bare land. This Council Tax is payable whether the house is occupied or not, and is levied on a sliding scale depending on the value (banding) of the property. The scale is different in each district and it therefore not possible to indicate the tax without knowing the property. Generally it is in the region of £1000 to £2000 per annum, but this is only a very rough guide.

Stamp duty is charged on your property at the same rates as in England and Wales. It is paid via your solicitor when you buy the property.

There is also a charge made for recording of your deeds on the Government land register, which is charged at the rate of £11 per £5,000 of value of the property.

Q. What kind of surveys are there?
A. As with England and Wales, there are three. The first is not a survey at all but a *Valuation*. It costs usually about £90 but is very limited in scope. It is usually prepared for a lender. If it is wrong you may have no comeback.

The second is a *Homebuyer's Report and Valuation*. This is much more detailed. It costs about £300 to £400. You have a direct relationship with the surveyor and if the survey is incorrect in a major way, then you will have an opportunity to make a claim on the insurance of the surveyor.

The third is a *Structural Survey,* but this is only normally instructed if the first survey indicates a serious problem. A structural survey can be quite expensive, depending upon the problem.

14
Questions, questions

This chapter deals with some typical scenarios arising from buying, selling and maintaining property.

I've been gazumped and lost money. Can I claim compensation? I recently made an offer for a house, and the seller's agent wrote to me saying his client had accepted the offer, subject to contract. I then spent money on a survey, bank costs, and legal costs. However, I later received a letter suggesting that the delay in getting a mortgage had caused the seller to 'review the situation'. Apparently he had received a higher offer but did not even give me the chance to meet it, which I would have done.

I took out a claim against the seller in the small claims court and received a letter from the seller's solicitor saying there is no claim under the Law of Property (Miscellaneous Provisions) Act 1989, where a contract is defined only in writing. Is there no recourse for costs suffered as a result of the seller's action?

The seller's solicitor is right. In these current overheated times, many people have been in this situation.

The Law of Property (Miscellaneous Provisions) Act was passed by Parliament to clarify the rules about when parties were legally bound and when they were not. It lays down certain formalities and if they are not complete, there is no binding legal relationship, and you would have no rights against the seller and vice versa.

A lockout agreement is a commonly-used way around this problem. This is a short document under which the seller agrees that, for an agreed time (such as one month), he or she will not negotiate with, or send out a contract to, anyone else. It does not commit either party to sell or buy. (For example, a buyer might not be able to raise a mortgage in time and the lockout would expire.) You should ask for a lockout agreement if you try to buy again.

I graduated four years ago, and am now studying to become a management accountant. I hope to be qualified within two years. I currently earn roughly £29k but expect my salary to rise quite a bit over the next few years. Are there any mortgage providers out there who'll take this into consideration and lend me more now? Basically, what is the most I can borrow?

With a 10 per cent deposit you could borrow up to four times your salary, so, assuming you have no outstanding loans or credit cards that could be deducted from the amount you could borrow, we are a looking at a mortgage of up to £116,000. Lenders usually do not take future earnings into consideration, but there are some who will look at affordability rather income multiples. This means you could, potentially, borrow the equivalent of four times your income with only a 5 per cent deposit. If you had a 15 per cent deposit, you could consider those lenders who offer mortgages based on 'self-certification' of income, which means that you can potentially borrow more than four times your income.

With all mortgages, and particularly self-certification, it is important to complete a monthly budget plan to make sure that you can afford the mortgage. The expectation of a large pay rise in two years may mean that all the extra expenditure of actually owning a property rather than renting, may make the mortgage too costly now. You may have a spare bedroom that you can let out and receive rent. Most lenders do not take rent into consideration, with the exception of Mortgage Express who do offer a specific 'rent-a-room' scheme that will take potential rental income into account when considering how much they would be willing to lend you. This may make all the difference to making the mortgage affordable to you.

Can taking out a loan make it more difficult to get a mortgage later? I am seriously considering consolidating debt into a loan in the region of £10,000 over a three- to five-year period. However, I am not yet on the mortgage ladder and am concerned how a debt of this size would affect any mortgage application.

I am self-employed, have three years' good accounts and credit history and would consider buying a property in a year or two.

A loan will usually affect how much you can borrow. A lender will normally add up the monthly repayments you make on loans, and then subtract this from your income before applying the normal mortgage income multiples. These vary, but a good figure to work with is 3.25 times annual income if you are buying on your own.

Some lenders will give up to four times annual income, others work on 'affordability' models rather than income multiples (IF.com and Standard Life are among the affordability lenders). This can work out more generously for you and the flexible mortgage deals offered by these lenders are often useful for the self-employed.

How do I buy an abandoned house? In my street there is a half-built property, which has been in this state for at least 10 years. The garden is fenced, but completely overgrown. The property is not registered with the Land Registry, and the local planners have no relevant records. This house does not officially exist.

I have been made aware of the rules of 'adverse possession' under which I could assume ownership after 12 years if I erected a fence around the house and maintained it. But I don't want to wait 12 years or raise the issue locally in case somebody else claims. What can I do? I would rather buy the property legally and quickly.

If the street was originally laid out by a developer or originally belonged to a landlord who later sold on the houses, you might be able to identify the original owner from old title deeds. They could include a record of the first buyer of the house. This may not help very much if the house has changed hands, but it could give you some guidance. The County Record Office is a good place to start looking.

Also, look at the deeds of the properties next to the house, which might include agreements about garden walls or common pipes. Old Post Office directories might also give a clue.

If a person dies with no relatives and no will, that is a matter for the Treasury solicitor at Queen Anne's Chambers, 28 Broadway, London SW1H 9JS.

Is my neighbour allowed to change my wall? I had a brick-built shed along the side of my garden, with a flat roof sloping towards the next garden and a rainwater gutter next to the neighbour's property to carry away water. There was a gap of four inches between the back wall of the shed and the boundary between the properties.

I removed the shed except for the back wall and hoped my neighbour would agree to my replacing that wall with a more attractive wall without a gutter. I wanted the wall to be set back slightly in order to cover the slip of land previously overhung by the shed gutter.

The neighbour refused, citing possible claims on the strip of ground. However, without permission he has removed the guttering from the remaining shed wall and has replaced it with a layer of rendering.

The changes do not affect my property or the appearance of my wall from our side. Yet I could be said to be losing the right to keep an untidy wall with a suspended gutter on it as a bargaining counter to persuade some future owner to accept the 'complete new wall' deal. Does the neighbour have the right to 'improve' my wall?

You remain owner of the gutter. You own the air space above it as a 'flying freehold'. The neighbour had no right to remove the guttering and you have the right to require him to pay the cost of installing a new one or, if he still has the gutter he removed, he must hand it over to you as your property. As the air space belongs to you it is up to you what gutter you fix, provided it does not extend further than the four inch strip.

The neighbour has possessory rights over the four-inch strip yielded because the shed wall was not on the exact boundary. If your neighbour has used the land as a flower bed, his rights may extend up to the typical heights of the flowers or shrubs growing there over the past 12 years.

Do I have to pay for my trees to be cut if they overhang a neighbour's garden? I have tall trees in my garden with some branches above our neighbour's garden. He wants to remove them, and I have told him he is welcome to do so. However, he says that, if he employs a tree surgeon, I should give him access to my garden and pay the bill. He says he will sue me if I don't pay. Does he have the right to claim money from me?

Your neighbour is free to cut the overhanging branches but at his expense. However, the branches remain your property, and he can insist you take them back, or pay for the part of the bill that relates to their disposal.

Can I transfer a mortgage indemnity premium? In 1997, I was a first-time buyer and was charged a mortgage indemnity premium (MIP) of more than £600. This was in respect of a 25-year repayment mortgage. Can I get any of this money back if I remortgage or can the premium be transferred to another mortgage provider?

The short answer is no. There's no way to recoup the cost of this 'hidden nasty'.

The longer explanation is that a MIP is charged by some lenders when borrowers want to borrow more than 90 per cent or 95 per cent of the value of a property. The one-off fee is used to buy insurance for the lender in case the borrower doesn't pay the mortgage and the lender has to repossess the property and sell it.

According to the Council of Mortgage Lenders: 'It is not usual for the high lending fee to be refunded either in full or in part, on early redemption of a mortgage, and the nature of these policies do not usually allow them to be transferred from one loan to another.'

MIPs are less common than they were in 1997, as many lenders have abandoned them due to adverse publicity. They offer no benefit at all to borrowers and should be avoided if at all possible.

The Council of Mortgage Lenders' website is at www.cml.org.uk.

How much would I expect to pay to extend my current lease, which is 61 years? The land has recently been sold to a new freeholder and I am worried if they can charge what they like.

I have instructed my solicitor to request the rights for me to extend the lease to pass onto my buyer. My buyer wants to know how much it is to extend before she exchanges contracts.

You can try to extend your lease voluntarily by contacting the new freeholder. You will need to agree a price with him. You will probably also need to pay his solicitor's costs and your own solicitor's costs, which are likely to be about £250 plus VAT and expenses.

If the new freeholder does not agree to extend your lease voluntarily then you may have the right to insist that he gives you a lease extension. The amount that you will have to pay to the new freeholder will depend upon a number of matters, ie value of property, length of lease, ground rent etc. Also you are likely to have to pay surveyor's fees, and the legal fees are likely to be considerably higher.

What is a 'flying freehold'? My husband and I own a property each – semi-detached chalet bungalows, which are next door to each other. Both are freehold mortgaged properties. We have made a modification whereby we have 'taken' part of the loft of one to give to next door (this enables us to gain easy access to loft space and therefore create another bedroom). This now protrudes over next door by about 5ft. I understand this has created a situation known as 'flying freehold', which apparently makes a property difficult to sell and to mortgage.

Who should we get to look at the properties to assess how much of a problem this is likely to create when we want to sell? Do the building societies that hold our mortgages need to be advised at this stage?

The issue we have here is that some banks\building societies will lend on properties with flying freeholds and others will not.

Those lenders that do lend on flying freeholds will do so only in certain circumstances and, in particular, where there exists all necessary rights of support protection and entry for repair, as well as a scheme of enforceable covenants that are also such that subsequent buyers are required to enter into covenants in identical form. If this clause cannot be complied with, then the lender may proceed in any event but only if indemnity insurance is obtained and in place on completion.

I am thinking of buying a two-bedroom converted first-floor flat in a mid-terraced house. If I bought the flat, I would share the freehold with the gentleman who owns the ground-floor flat.

I am aware that flats that have share of freehold can be potentially troublesome when it comes to paying for repairs to the building (for example the roof). I asked the owner what the arrangements were and she said that, as far as she is aware, any such cost would be split two ways with the owner of the ground-floor flat. However, she did not seem certain of this.

Should there be some sort of legal agreement with whoever the freehold is shared with? If so, what should I be looking for in such an agreement? It also occurred to me that there may be potential issues with the flats and/or houses that are either side of the property (in the event of subsidence, etc). Can you give me any advice as to what I should be looking for in this respect?

It is very much better to have a share in the freehold than not. There is only a potential problem if there has not been a separate lease granted in respect of each flat – but usually there has. In any event this can easily be resolved.

An agreement can be drawn up between each owner but it is probably not necessary – in a block of two flats things can usually be agreed without too much formality. By owning a share in the freehold you will avoid any potential disputes with a freeholder and/or managing agent. Also there is no worry about extending the lease if the term is getting shorter.

Will we have problems selling our property because of old alterations? We have a through lounge, which was carried out prior to when we purchased our house some 12 years ago. Will we have problems because no building regulation consent was obtained?

Also, three years ago we had a garage erected at the bottom of our 125 ft garden. We were told by the company that erected it that planning permission was not required. Is that true? Will we have problems, as we are planning to sell our property?

So far as the through lounge is concerned, you should not have any problems when you come to sell your property because the work was carried out more than 12 years ago. However, because of a recent change in the law, it may be that the solicitors acting for a buyer of your property will be concerned about the lack of building regulation consent.

If this occurs, then you can arrange for the local buildings inspector to re-inspect with a view to giving retrospective consent, or for a very modest premium, you can obtain a lack of building regulation consent indemnity policy.

So far as the garage is concerned, whether or not you require planning permission and/or building regulation consent will depend upon a number of matters, ie nature of construction, size of garage etc. We suggest that you contact your local planning authority now to find out from them their guidelines for planning permission for garages. If planning permission was required, then, again, you can apply for retrospective planning consent. Alternatively, a buyer may be prepared to proceed on the basis that the garage is now more than three years old and no enforcement proceedings have been started.

I took out a mortgage just over a year ago and it is fixed until August this year (2003) at 5.65 per cent. I would like to move house (up the ladder) at the end of the fixed term. I have just inherited some money that I could use to take 10 years off my mortgage but I still do not want to move until August 2003. Do I hold on to the money and then up it in August 2003 or re-negotiate my mortgage and pay penalties?

The answer to this really depends on two things – your tax rate and the redemption penalties. For example, let's assume your outstanding mortgage is for £50,000. If you were to pay the penalty now, and for argument's sake let's assume the penalty equates to six months' interest, then you would have to pay a penalty of £1,412 to free yourself from this mortgage.

If you opted to wait until the fixed rate period expired, and therefore put this money in some sort of savings account until then, you need to compare the amount of interest you will receive in the savings account to how much interest you would pay on the mortgage (also taking into account the assumed £1,412 you would have to pay to redeem the mortgage). This is where your tax rate comes into the equation. Because interest on a savings account is taxed, it will make a difference to your decision if you are a higher-rate tax payer.

I suggest you consult an independent financial adviser. With access to the full details they would be able to make an informed decision as to which option is most financially suitable to you.

I earn about £15,000 a year and would like to buy my own place. What is on offer for such a low wage?

You could potentially borrow up to four times your gross salary, therefore assuming you earn £15,000 before tax, you could potentially borrow £60,000.

If we also assume you have savings that amount to a 10 per cent deposit you could potentially buy a property worth £66,000. This may well be enough depending on where and what you want to buy. However, it is based on a number of assumptions such as you having no outstanding debt that could reduce your borrowing power, you have saved up at least a 10 per cent deposit and also have extra money to cover your purchase costs.

In order to increase your borrowing power there are other options that you could consider, such as lenders who base their decision on a borrower's affordability rather than set income multiples, or lenders who offer 100 per cent mortgages, thus negating the need for a deposit.

I suggest you seek independent advice to see if any of these options are suitable for you. With more information to work on, an independent adviser should be able to work out the best option for you, including whether you should be thinking of buying at all.

Is it possible to obtain a joint 100 per cent mortgage, ie with no deposit? A flatmate and I are considering a joint mortgage application to avoid wasting money on rent. I have money for a deposit, my flatmate does not.

In this instance, and for simplicity, can a joint 100 per cent mortgage be obtained? We are both in permanent employment.

It is possible for you both to get a 100 per cent mortgage but the bigger issue here is ensuring you both understand exactly what you are about to undertake. While friends buying together has become a more popular way for first-time buyers to get on the property ladder as prices soar, you both need to be aware of the risks involved before committing to buying a property together.

The main risk is what will happen if one of you decides to move out, falls on hard times or even dies. All parties on the mortgage deed will be jointly and severally liable to pay the mortgage, and if any of these scenarios should happen, it may fall on the other co-owner to make up the balance of the mortgage payments. Whether or not the increased payments are manageable may depend on how far down the line this happens, as financial circumstances will obviously change over time.

A good safeguard is to draw up a legal agreement to cover these eventualities before the purchase is completed. It should take into account how much you are both putting into the property, both in terms of any deposit you initially put down and the various costs of purchase.

Although only one of you has money for a deposit I still think it is worthwhile using it for this purpose, as long as it is at least 5 per cent of the purchase price. This is because it will enable you to choose from a much wider range of lenders and mortgages, and consequently you will both benefit by being able to get a lower interest rate. Although, as far as the lender is concerned you will both be equally responsible for making the mortgage payments but you can, if you wish, split the payments unevenly between yourselves if, for example, you provide all of the deposit. This is one of the reasons why it is so important for you both to agree in writing beforehand what proportion of the mortgage and household bills you each pay and how the proceeds will be split if and when you sell. This should ensure that there is no dispute in the future as to what each party is entitled to if and when it comes to buying a co-owner out or selling the property.

You should both independently seek advice from a solicitor (and this should not be the same solicitor, although two solicitors from the same firm would be OK) before you commit to anything.

We are buying a brand new house and we are trying to sort out our finances. We want to know whether or not we can have a mortgage offer now, which will be valid for our purchase even though the house will not be completed for another six months.

Yes, you can. Most mortgage offers are valid for a period of three to six months, so this may mean that you will have to renew your offer, which typically involves the lender getting an updated credit search and proof of your earnings. Be mindful though because even though you may chose a particular mortgage deal now, it may have expired by the time your house is ready. You should take care to check this with the lender, as some schemes have deadlines by which the mortgage must be drawn down.

I live in a Victorian house with cellars that I would like to use for extra living space. The cellars themselves are not totally underground. Only about 4ft of the cellars are. I have put windows in and I am putting in forced-air ventilation to the outside. The cellars have asphalt floors and the walls have been dampcoursed. There are only two walls that give me cause for concern, because they back on to the front gardens and only the bottom 4ft has signs of damp. All the other walls are fine.

I don't really want to dig out the front gardens and treat the walls from the outside because that would be very time-consuming and impractical. Can I treat the problem walls from the inside to stop damp and the smell of damp from penetrating inside. I have been advised to apply rot-proof roofing felt bonded with cold asphalt to the affected walls and continued to the floor to give an effective seal. Would this work? Are there any other alternatives? I did apply Cellar Paint to the walls some years ago but that has peeled off.

What you have to bear in mind is that any below-ground walls will always be prone to lateral groundwater penetration. Tanking the walls on the inside may stop the water showing on the decorative surfaces, but the brickwork itself will still be saturated, and the moisture will be trapped behind the tanking. This usually results in humid, smelly conditions.

The first thing you should do is to find out why the front walls are wetter than the others. It may be that the rainwater down-pipe from the roof is not connected up to the main drains, but is discharging into the ground. Victorian houses often had two separate drainage systems, with foul water (sewage) going into the drains, and rainwater going into 'soak-aways', which were holes in the ground next to the basement walls. It may be that diverting this water away to the drains will solve 90 per cent of your dampness problems.

After that, digging a trench and waterproofing the wall on the outside is by far the best option. But if you really want to try and keep the water at bay from the inside, then you need a drained ventilated membrane system such as Platon (from Triton Chemicals Ltd, 020 8310 3929) or Newlath (from John Newton & Co, 020 7237 1217). These can be finished internally by plastering or panelling.

I'd like to have a shower in my bathroom but the water pressure is very low upstairs. Are there any ways round this?

You don't say whether you are talking about low mains pressure or low pressure from a storage tank. If the former, then the first thing to do is check with your water supplier what the pressure should be in your area, and that you are not restricting this with narrow-bore pipework. But the usual problem in upstairs bathrooms is that the water storage tank is only a few centimetres higher than the shower outlet, giving only a small 'head' of pressure. Again, you should first check that the pipes are not blocked or scaled up, and that the hot and cold feeds from the tank to the bathroom (including the hot flow through the heater or cylinder) are all in 22 mm pipe, rather than 15 mm.

Assuming all these are in order, and the pressure is still low, then the answer is to fit an electric shower booster pump. These can be either twin-port – boosting both hot and cold supplies from the existing plumbing system – or single-port, which will provide a boosted cold supply for an 'instant' electric shower unit. These are fairly simple devices, and can be fitted by keen DIYers, but if you are not confident of your plumbing skills, you would be well advised to have the pump fitted by a professional plumbing and heating engineer, and the electrics should be installed or approved by an NICEIC registered electrician.

We live in a 1920s semi and every year gusts of wind dislodge one or two roof slates. The roof is in its original 1920s condition with no underfelt. There are adverts in the papers for a 'foam spray solution' for old roofs. These are guaranteed for 20 or so years. Is this the easiest way forward, or should we look to get the whole roof redone? I have heard conflicting reports about the foam-type repair, varying from 'fantastic' to 'waste of money'. As the damage is only slight each year, would it be better to just keep on repairing the occasional damage instead?

The fact that slates are slipping every year indicates that the nails which hold them to the timber battens are rusted through, and it is time to have the roof stripped off and re-covered. Having foam sprayed onto the undersides of the slates may sound like a wonderful high-tech solution but it is a bad idea. It is at odds with the recommendations of the Building Regulations, which require a clear 50 mm ventilated gap between insulation and roof covering. The foam sets hard and removes the two vital attributes of a traditional roof, which are the ability to breathe and to move. The foam covers the battens and the top surfaces of the rafters, which could lead to them rot. It also sticks tight to the slates and makes it almost impossible for them to ever be re-used. You will also probably find that the cost of the spray-on foam solution will be three or four times that of having the roof re-covered in the traditional way. Try to find a roofer who will remove the existing slates carefully and re-use as many as possible.

Several of my double-glazed windows have misted up between the panes. The double-glazing was already installed when I bought the house and the estate agent's particulars implied that this was a good thing. But on the south-facing side of the house (overlooking the garden), on a sunny day, I can hardly see out of the windows because of the misting. Is there anything that can be done to cure this, or, if I have the double-glazing replaced, is there any way of ensuring that it does not happen in the future?

Sealed double-glazed units (SGUs) are always prone to misting up. Manufacturers postpone the inevitable by incorporating a desiccant material in the perforated alloy strip that runs around the edges between the two panes of glass. But eventually the desiccant will become saturated, and then misting is inevitable. How long this takes depends upon a number of factors – if the SGUs are manufactured and installed to the correct British Standards, then they should last at least 20 years. But for this to happen, the SGUs must be mounted in drained, ventilated rebates in the window frames, so that no moisture is allowed to come into contact with the edges of the glass. Unfortunately, most 'double-glazing' is supplied and installed by companies who do not understand these principles, and SGUs are often fixed tight into PVCU frames or even sealed in with mastic or putty into timber or alloy frames. In these circumstances misting can occur within a few years, or even months of installation.

I live in a basement flat in a Victorian house and am besieged by noise – traffic outside, music from either side, and the footsteps of the people upstairs. What can I do to make my life quieter?

The best way to cut down traffic noise is to fit secondary glazing. This is not to be confused with double-glazing, which has a 3 or 4 mm air gap between the two panes of glass, and is good for thermal insulation. Secondary glazing has a much bigger air gap – 200 mm is the optimum – and will reduce traffic noise by up to two-thirds. For best results, make sure you thoroughly draught-proof the existing windows at the same time, as air-borne sound travels through gaps.

Something of the same philosophy applies to noise from your next-door neighbours – if you can smell their cooking then you will also be able to hear their TV – so locating and plugging gaps in the party walls can do a lot to cut down unwanted noise intrusion.

The most difficult problem is the footsteps from the neighbours above. Ideally, this involves constructing a new floor – separated by sound-proofing quilt – on top of the existing floor in their flat. A less satisfactory alternative is to build a false ceiling in the lower flat. You can download information on improving sound insulation from the Building Research Establishment website.

Last winter I had trouble with frozen pipes and water tanks in my roof space. How can I make sure this does not happen again, and are there any other precautions that I should take when the cold weather approaches?

Pipes and tanks freezing in roof spaces is an inevitable result of the high levels of insulation that we now have in our homes. Water tanks are kept up in the loft because it is a convenient place to have them, and because the height provides a good head of pressure that allows water to flow by gravity to kitchen and bathroom taps. But because most homes now have a thick layer of insulation quilt between the top-floor ceiling joists, very little heat escapes up into the roof space, and so on cold winter nights the temperature can easily fall below freezing.

Apart from the inconvenience of having the water supply cut off, the main problem with freezing water is that as it freezes it also expands, and so can damage the plumbing. The resulting leak is often inaccurately referred to as a 'burst pipe', but a burst or split in a straight run of copper pipe is rare. What usually happens is that the expanding ice pushes compression joints open – such as those that connect pipes to tanks. Should this happen, by the way, you should always check to see whether the fitting can be pushed back into place and re-tightened, before panicking and calling out the emergency plumber.

Preventing this situation is achieved by making sure that loft insulation goes over, rather than under, pipes and tanks, thus keeping them at house temperature. If this is not possible, then a small electric heater with a 'frost' setting on the thermostat can be set up in the loft.

Other weak points are outside taps and lavatory cisterns. These should be isolated by cheap on/off valves ('ball-o-fix' or similar), which can be turned on and off with a screwdriver. Turn them off when freezing weather threatens, and leave the taps open and cisterns empty until warm conditions return.

15
Useful contacts

Property websites

www.asserta.co.uk

www.easier.co.uk

www.fish4homes.co.uk

www.homes-on-line.com

www.homepages.co.uk

www.hometrack.co.uk

www.new-homes.co.uk

www.propertymarket.co.uk

www.propertyfinder.co.uk

www.propertyworld.co.uk

www.rightmove.co.uk

www.upmysreet.co.uk

Organisations

Architectural Association
36 Bedford Square
London WC1B 3ES
Tel: 020 7887 4000
Fax: 020 7414 0782
Website: www.arch-assoc.org.uk

Architecture and Surveying Institute
St Mary House
15A St Mary Street
Chippenham
Wiltshire SN15 3WD
Tel: 01249 444505
Fax: 01249 443602
Website: www.asi.org.uk

Association of British Insurers
51 Gresham Street
London EC2V 7HQ
Tel: 020 7600 3333
Fax: 020 7696 8999
Website: www.abi.org.uk

Association of Building Engineers
Lutyens House
Billing Brook Road
Weston Favell
Northampton NN3 8NW
Tel: 01604 404121
Fax: 01604 784220

Association of Plumbing and Heating Contractors
Ensign House
Ensign Business Centre
Westwood Way
Coventry CV4 8JA
Tel: 0800 542 6060
Fax: 024 7647 0942
Website: www.licensedplumber.co.uk

Association of Relocation Agents
PO Box 189
Diss
Norfolk IP22 1PE
Tel: 08700 737475
Fax: 08700 718719
Website: www.relocationagents.com

British Association of Removers
3 Churchill Court
58 Station Road
North Harrow
Middlesex HA2 7SA
Tel: 020 8861 3331
Fax: 020 8861 3332
Website: www.barmovers.com

British Insurance Brokers' Association
BIBA House
14 Bevis Marks
London EC3A 7NT
Tel: 020 7623 9043
Fax: 020 7626 9676
Website: www.biba.org.uk

Building Societies Association
3 Savile Row
London W1S 3PB
Tel: 020 7437 0655
Fax: 020 7734 6416
Website: www.bsa.org.uk

Construction Confederation
Construction House
56–64 Leonard Street
London EC2A 4JX
Tel: 020 7608 5000
Fax: 020 7608 5001
Website: www.thecc.org.uk

The Controller of Stamps
London Stamp Office
South West Wing
Bush House
Strand
London WC2B 4QN
Tel: Helpline 0845 6030 135
Fax: 020 7438 7302
Website: www.inlandrevenue.gov.uk/so

Council for Licensed Conveyancers
16 Glebe Road
Chelmsford
Essex CM1 1QG
Tel: 01245 349599
Fax: 01245 341300
Website: www.conveyancer.org.uk

Council for Registered Gas Installers (CORGI)
Unit 1 Elmwood
Chineham Park
Basingstoke
Hampshire RG24 8WG
Tel: 01256 372200
Fax: 01256 708144
Website: www.corgi-gas.com

Council of Mortgage Lenders
3 Savile Row
London W1S 3PB
Tel: 020 7437 0075
Fax: 020 7434 3791
Website: www.cml.org.uk

Electrical Contractors' Association
ESCA House
34 Palace Court
London W2 4HY
Tel: 020 7313 4800
Fax: 020 7221 7344
Website: www.eca.co.uk

English Heritage
Customer Services Department
PO Box 569
Swindon SN2 2YP
Tel: 0870 333 1181
Fax: 01793 414926
Website: www.english-heritage.org.uk

Federation of Master Builders
14–15 Great James Street
London WC1N 3DP
Tel: 020 7242 7583
Fax: 020 7404 0296
Website: www.fmb.org.uk

The Institute of Plumbing
64 Station Lane
Hornchurch
Essex RM12 6NB
Tel: 01708 472791
Fax: 01708 448987
Website: www.plumbers.org.uk

The Law Commission
Conquest House
37–38 John Street
Theobalds Road
London WC1N 2BQ
Tel: 020 7453 1220
Fax: 020 7453 1297
Website: www.lawcom.gov.uk

The Law Society
113 Chancery Lane
London WC2A 1PL
Tel: 020 7242 1222
Fax: 020 7831 0344
Website: www.lawsociety.org.uk

The Law Society of Scotland
26 Drumsheugh Gardens
Edinburgh EH3 7YR
Tel: 0131 226 7411
Fax: 0131 225 2934
Website: www.lawscot.org.uk

Legal Services Ombudsman
1st Floor
Sunlight House
Quay Street
Manchester M3 3JZ
Tel: 0161 839 7262
Fax: 0161 832 5446
Website: www.olso.org

National Approval Council for Security Systems (NACOSS)
Queensgate House
14 Cookham Road
Maidenhead
Berkshire SL6 8AJ
Tel: 01628 637512
Fax: 01628 773367
Website: www.nsi.org.uk

The National Association of Estate Agents (NAEA)
Arbon House
21 Jury Street
Warwick
Warwickshire CV34 4EH
Tel: 01926 496800
Fax: 01926 400953
Website: www.propertylive.co.uk

National Guild of Removers and Storers
3 High Street
Chesham
Buckinghamshire HP5 1BG
Tel: 01494 792279
Fax: 01494 792111
Website: www.ngrs.co.uk

National House Building Council (NHBC)
Buildmark House
Chiltern Avenue
Amersham
Buckinghamshire HP6 5AP
Tel: 01494 434477
Fax: 01494 735201
Website: www.nhbc.co.uk

New Homes Marketing Board (NHMB)
56–64 Leonard Street
London EC2A 4JX
Tel: 020 7608 5100
Fax: 020 7608 5101
Website: www.new-homes.co.uk

Office of the Ombudsman for Estate Agents (OEA)
Beckett House
4 Bridge Street
Salisbury
Wiltshire SP1 2LX
Tel: 01722 333306
Fax: 01722 332296
Website: www.org.co.uk

Office for the Supervision of Solicitors (OSS)
Victoria Court
8 Dormer Place
Leamington Spa
Warwickshire CV32 5AE
Tel: 01926 820082
Fax: 01926 431435
Website: www.lawsociety.org.uk

Registry of County Court Judgements
Registry Trust Ltd
173–175 Cleveland Street
London W1P 5PE
Tel: 020 7380 0133

The Royal Incorporation of Architects in Scotland (RIA Scotland)
15 Rutland Square
Edinburgh EH1 2BE
Tel: 0131 229 7545
Fax: 0131 228 2188
Website: www.rias.org.uk

Royal Institute of British Architects (RIBA)
Client Services
66 Portland Place
London W1B 1AD
Tel: 020 7580 5533
Fax: 020 7255 1541
Website: www.architecture.com

Royal Institution of Chartered Surveyors (RICS)
RICS Contact Centre
Surveyor Court
Westwood Way
Coventry CV4 8JE
Tel: 0870 333 1600
Website: www.rics.org.uk

Royal Institution of Chartered Surveyors in Scotland (RICS Scotland)
9 Manor Place
Edinburgh EH3 7DN
Tel: 0131 225 7078
Fax: 0131 240 0830
Website: www.rics-scotland.org.uk

Royal Society of Architects in Wales
Bute Building
King Edward VII Avenue
Cathays Park
Cardiff CF10 3NB
Tel: 029 2087 4753
Fax: 029 2087 4926
Website: www.architecture-wales.com

Royal Society of Ulster Architects (RSUA)
2 Mount Charles
Belfast BT7 1NZ
Tel: 028 9032 3760
Fax: 028 9023 7313
Website: www.rsua.org.uk

Royal Town Planning Institute
41 Botolph Lane
London EC3R 8DL
Tel: 020 7929 9494
Fax: 020 7929 9490
Website: www.rtpi.org.uk

Scottish Building
Carron Grange
Carrongrange Avenue
Stenhousemuir FK5 3BQ
Tel: 01324 555550
Fax: 01324 555551
Website: www.scottish-building.co.uk

The Scottish Civic Trust
The Tobacco Merchants House
42 Miller Street
Glasgow G1 1DT
Tel: 0141 221 1466
Fax: 0141 248 6952
Website www.scotnet.co.uk/sct

The Society for the Protection of Ancient Buildings
37 Spital Square
London E1 6DY
Tel: 020 7377 1644
Fax: 020 7247 5296
Website www.spab.org.uk

The Stationary Office (TSO)
Duke Street
PO Box 29
Norwich NR3 1GN
Tel: 0870 600 5522
Fax: 0870 600 5533
Website: www.tso.co.uk

Zurich Municipal
Galaxy House
Southwood Crescent
Farnborough
Hampshire GU14 0NJ
Tel: 01252 522000
Fax: 01252 372989
Website: www.zurich.com

Index of advertisers